T0227868

Project Management Case Studies and Lessons Learned

Stakeholder, Scope, Knowledge, Schedule, Resource and Team Management

Project Management Case Studies and Lessons Learned

Stakeholder, Scope, Knowledge, Schedule, Resource and Team Management

M. Kemal Atesmen

CRC Press
Taylor & Francis Group
Boca Raton London New York

CRC Press is an imprint of the
Taylor & Francis Group, an **informa** business
AN AUERBACH BOOK

CRC Press
Taylor & Francis Group
6000 Broken Sound Parkway NW, Suite 300
Boca Raton, FL 33487-2742

First issued in hardback 2017

ISBN 13: 978-1-138-42318-3 (hbk)
ISBN 13: 978-1-4987-0040-5 (pbk)

Library of Congress Cataloging-in-Publication Data

Atesmen, M. Kemal.
    Project management case studies and lessons learned : stakeholder, scope, knowledge, schedule, resource, and team management / M. Kemal Atesmen.
        pages cm
    Summary: "Based on the author's 35 years of experience in project management, this book is filled with case studies and lessons learned on managing project stakeholders, teams, resources, and schedules. The aim of the book is to help project managers with solutions to common project problems. It also helps project managers to gain insight into crafting solutions to unique challenges in managing projects. This book is especially helpful to project managers whose teams are globally dispersed and present challenges based on cultural differences"-- Provided by publisher.
    Includes bibliographical references and index.
    ISBN 978-1-4987-0040-5 (pbk.)
    1. Project management. 2. Industrial management. I. Title.

HD69.P75.A84 2014
658.4'04--dc23

2014039475

Visit the Taylor & Francis Web site at
http://www.taylorandfrancis.com

and the CRC Press Web site at
http://www.crcpress.com

Contents

Preface

As global project managers we continually have to fight against ever-changing currents of project stakeholder management, scope management, knowledge management, schedule management, resource management, and above all team management. As global project managers we have to strategize and find plausible solutions in a timely fashion to all events that endanger our project's feasible direction. Finding timely solutions to challenging events becomes more difficult in a global project environment.

In this book, I outline 82 challenging cases that I encountered during my global project management career all over the world. I analyze each case by detailing the issue, how I strategized and approached it for a solution, what the solution was, and what I learned from that case. As I became more experienced in project management, the quantity of challenging events in a project decreased. Lessons learned from each surprising event or personal mistake transformed me into a more careful and more detailed project manager. The benefits from this book can make a global project manager more proactive, more careful, more disciplined, and ready for sudden and similar surprises that can affect his or her project. Project cases detailed in this book will support and guide your strategizing process during the execution of global projects. Lessons learned are summarized after every case.

Challenging cases detailed in this book in a global project environment cover stakeholder management issues, scope management issues, knowledge management issues, schedule management issues, resource management issues, and team management issues.

M. Kemal Atesmen
Santa Barbara, California

Acknowledgments

Over 33 years of engineering project management in the global arena covering automotive, computer, data communication, and offshore oil industries was accomplished with exceptional support from my wife, Zeynep, and my family members. Some years I was away from home for more than six months out of a year trying to tackle challenging project tasks.

I would like to dedicate this book to all project team members with whom I had the pleasure of working with over the years, who did the hard work with enthusiasm, and who kept coming back to work along with me on a project team without any reservations.

About the Author

M. Kemal Atesmen completed his high school studies at Robert Academy in Istanbul, Turkey in 1961. He received his B.Sc. degree from Case Western Reserve University, his M.Sc. degree from Stanford University, and his Ph.D. degree from Colorado State University, all in mechanical engineering. He is a life member of ASME. He initially pursued an academic and an industrial career in parallel and became an associate professor in mechanical engineering before dedicating his professional life to international engineering project management and engineering management for 33 years. He helped many young engineers in the international arena to bridge the gap between college and professional life in automotive, computer component, data communication, and offshore oil industries.

Dr. Atesmen has published five books, 16 technical papers, and has four patents. His books include: *Global Engineering Project Management* (CRC Press, 2008); *Everyday Heat Transfer Problems—Sensitivities to Governing Variables* (ASME Press, 2009); *Understanding the World Around Through Simple Mathematics* (Infinity Publishing, 2011); and *A Journey Through Life* (Wilson Printing, 2013).

Introduction

I published a book entitled *Global Engineering Project Management* in 2008. This book covered bidding, planning, executing, and closure phases of global engineering project management. However, it did not detail solutions to unusual, unexpected, and challenging events that I encountered during my 33 years of global engineering project management in automotive, computer component, data communication, and offshore oil industries.

A project is a six-legged structure. Each leg can be characterized by a project's stakeholders, a project's scope, a project's knowledge base, a project's schedule, a project's resources including its budget, and a project's team. If one of these legs starts to wobble or starts to show cracks, the whole project becomes unstable and runs into hard times. As project managers we are the ultimate strategists. We have to manage appropriately our project's stakeholders. We have to understand all pertinent specifications and be on top of all scope changes. We have to watch and control the project schedule like a hawk. We have to be on top of all tasks and especially the critical ones. I have seen very few projects that were completed on schedule and within budget during my career. We have to sort out missed schedules and budget targets with our upper management and with our customers. We have to strategize and use resources available to us wisely. The most important and valuable leg of our project structure is our project team. We have to treat our team members with consideration and respect. We have to understand what motivates them. We have to lead them by applying appropriate vigor. We have to help them solve all their issues.

A strong project manager has vision, perspective, and judgment to strategize where the problems are going to happen and takes timely steps to prevent damage to his project's structure. Sometimes unexpected surprises and catastrophes occur during the life of a project. Then as project managers, we have to marshal all of our resourcefulness and management skills to achieve viable solutions.

This book is about surprising, unexpected, and catastrophic cases that I had to live through during my global project management career. I extracted 82 challenging cases that affected every leg of my projects' structures. I explain each challenging case and then how I went about remedying the issue at hand. Some cases involved a logical step-by-step approach toward a solution. Some cases required unorthodox steps to get the project on the right track. Lessons learned are summarized after every case.

Your project's stakeholders can hamper or contribute to the progress of your project tremendously. In Chapter 1, I present 22 challenging project cases that are related to my stakeholders' actions.

Your project's scope can change direction suddenly and impact the progress of your project. In Chapter 2, I outline eight unexpected cases affecting my projects' scopes during my global engineering project management career.

Your team's and resource's knowledge can also hamper or contribute to the progress of your project tremendously. In Chapter 3, I have 11 challenging project cases that are related to my projects' knowledge base management.

Your project's schedule management requires constant focus and scrutiny. In Chapter 4, I have six such challenging project cases that are related to my projects' schedule performance.

Your project resources can affect the progress of your project tremendously. I had several unexpected cases regarding my project's resources including its budget during my global engineering project management career. In Chapter 5, I present 14 challenging project cases that are related to my projects' resources.

Your project team is the most important leg of your project management structure. Any weakness in this structure will definitely degrade your project's performance. You have to do all you can to keep your team under control and make them perform to their highest level of capabilities. In Chapter 6, I outline 21 challenging cases related to my projects' teams.

1

CASE STUDIES IN STAKEHOLDER MANAGEMENT

Stakeholders that can affect your project can vary from your customer(s), your company, your project partner(s), your company's investors, to your subcontractors. During the course of your global project, you have to manage all these entities as needed.

Health of the cash flow in your company can be a project derailing factor as it happened to me in Case 1.1. Changing and condensing the project schedule in order to help my company to get paid two weeks earlier was a challenging eye opener for me.

Protecting the intellectual property of my company during technology transfer to a Japanese company was a very challenging project assignment to me as detailed in Case 1.2. Detailed preparations and training of my people before Japanese engineers invaded my company's facilities were key elements for the project's success.

Our corporate closed down our company's operations during the 2000 to 2002 dot-com bust. I was right in the middle of a data communication chip design project. My team and I had to jump over hoops and had to make lots of sacrifices, but we held together as a team in order to complete our project successfully. This challenging event is detailed in Case 1.3.

As travel costs for an internal project to Malaysia skyrocketed, my travel budget was frozen by my company's upper management. My team and I took many steps to curb our travel costs. I pleaded with my upper management for my project's travel budget increase. Every time I was rejected. They emphasized that I should cut down on travel and keep my travel budget as it was. We did all we could as shown in Case 1.4, but in the end we still exceeded our travel budget.

During a project every member of my team reported to their particular department's manager and reported to me on a dotted line basis. I had no control of their performance reviews, promotions, salary increases, training, and personal issues. One day I lost the services of our whole quality department. I had to scramble to find replacements without hampering the progress of my project as described in Case 1.5.

I was given the internal project of putting together an extensive feasibility study in three months in order to give direction to our magnetic head manufacturing processes for the next generation of our products. There were three different approaches in three different countries that were being considered by different groups in my company. I detailed the actions I took to generate the feasibility study and the final decision process in Case 1.6.

Upper management changes in a company can impact positively or negatively internal project directions, project teams, management styles, and project reporting styles. Personnel and responsibility changes in upper management and on my team caused tsunami effects to my project. I outlined these effects in Case 1.7.

A project manager has to fully understand at the beginning of the project all contract agreement conditions for delays in deliveries, patents, copyrights, trademarks, force majeure, subcontracting rules and governing laws, and arbitration. In addition to understanding all contract agreement conditions, he has to relay them to his team members in layman's terms. Our legal department saved my bacon from a dispute that arose at the end of a project with my customer as detailed in Case 1.8.

Salary and compensation variations in a multinational company can cause stress, disputes, and jealousy in an internal project team environment. Team members have to be very sensitive and careful not to discuss salary and compensation issues with each other locally or internationally. Such a flare-up is discussed in Case 1.9.

Lessons learned from previous projects within a company let a project manager start his or her project on a strong footing. Undocumented historical projects and uncontrolled lessons learned items create a large vacuum for a project manager. Such an occurrence is detailed in Case 1.10.

A company's upper management cannot decide on the future direction of the company internally by themselves. They mostly go outside to get help. They approach consulting firms, experts in their field, even friends outside the company in order to get a fresh outlook and ideas for the future of their company as shown in Case 1.11.

Your customer(s) are crucial stakeholders in your project. You have to do all you can to manage your customer(s) too. In order to ease tensions between my Korean engineering project team and my Japanese customer's visiting qualification team, I decided to go to Korea first for two weeks to prepare and train my Korean team for our Japanese customer's qualification process both psychologically and technically. Historical animosities between two countries can affect the progress of a project. Preparing carefully for such complicated encounters between project's parties is described in Case 1.12.

A customer placed a resident engineer into my project group in the United States to oversee all our activities and to make sure that their intellectual properties were fully protected. The customer also assigned a resident engineer to our volume production plant in South Korea. This resident engineer also traveled to Japan to check on our subcontractor every fortnight. Complications that were encountered during the execution of my project with two resident engineers are detailed in Case 1.13.

I could never close out a project because the final project evaluation by the customer's project manager was missing. I had to jump through many hoops in order to get my customer's final project evaluation report as detailed in Case 1.14.

Communicating filtered information is the backbone of a project's control structure. How much information to pass on and how much you want to disturb the cart are crucial factors during the life of a project. If every little detail regarding your project goes to your customer, you are mismanaging your project. You have to filter out ripples in your communicated information. At the same time you have to realize what information and when to inform your customer without any delay. Such challenges were encountered in Case 1.15.

For a global project manager, keeping track of all national and religious holidays of countries that you are dealing with are a requirement. You have to also know religious beliefs of every individual you are dealing with in order not to run into surprises as depicted in Case 1.16.

I received a call from my customer's project manager that the project goods' shipment arrived safely in South Korea, but they could not clear the cargo from South Korean customs because the spare parts were missing from the final inspection report's packing list. The customer's inspectors, the customer's bank, and my shipping department all missed the 10 spare parts from the packing list. This incomplete packing list caused me a lot of headaches as shown in Case 1.17.

In every project, almost all hands in a company swarm around a critical project person with good intentions to get a feeling of how things are going. They waste his or her valuable time. If the project person has an easygoing personality, he or she tries to accommodate everyone's inquiries and questions. Valuable time can be wasted and the project schedule can unintentionally go down the drain. You have to caution your team members to let you know if there are unnecessary interferences with their work. As a project manager, you have to protect your team members from these unnecessary distractions as depicted in Case 1.18.

I had a distasteful ordeal with an authoritarian director during one of my projects. Case 1.19 details the events that occurred during an unfortunate management clash.

After 14 months of challenging problem-solving sessions, board meetings, communications, and travels between our U.S. plant in California, our subcontractor in Boston, and our plant in Malaysia, my project team, our subcontractor, and the Malaysian project team had continual changes in every task of a challenging project to implement two automation assembly modules in our Malaysian plant as detailed in Case 1.20.

Closing a project appropriately can be painful and time consuming for a project manager. However, the rewards for a properly closed project can be invaluable for your team members and for your company. Lessons learned tasks are the most important ones on a project's closure to-do list. As project managers we have to finalize lessons learned tasks at all cost as detailed in Case 1.21.

Everyone on our team and every member of our company's upper management has to understand the penalties involved in a project's contract. Late deliveries and resulting price reductions in a contract's value and also resulting liquidated damages can damage a company irreversibly. Such cases are detailed in Case 1.22.

Case 1.1: Company Cash Flow Issue Affecting Design Review Pull-In

In the middle of an equipment design, build, and test project for an offshore oil platform, the company president came to my office and explained to me that the company had a shortage in cash flow during the coming months. He asked me if I could bring in the customer design review and design drawings approval phase of my project, which was due in eight weeks, by two weeks so that the company could get paid 10% of the total project funding two weeks earlier. I told the company president that I would work on his request with my team members and with the customer's project manager and get back to him in three working days.

This was quite a challenge that was thrown in my lap on top of all my other project management responsibilities. The company president's request went to the top of my action item list because the company's cash flow health meant a lot to the morale of my team members and to myself. Another twist on this issue was the inner workings of our customer who was Finnish. This was our first project for them. I had no idea if the customer's project manager and finance department would entertain such an earlier design review and phase 1 payment to us. My team had to design, check, and release close to 40 drawings, 15 calculations, a structural interface drawing approved by the customer, and the control panel software code before the design review meeting. We had to cut our task's duration by 25%.

The first step was to discuss the situation with my team members. I had a team meeting with them the next day. I explained to them the company president's request to accelerate the first phase of our project by two weeks. I had six full time engineers working on the project. We went over every task, 140 of them, that had to be completed and over all the task interactions. The team members had good suggestions.

One of them was to bring into our project a senior engineer from the manufacturing department full time for six weeks to check the design calculations and drawings.

Another suggestion was to get two more workstations assigned by the IT department full time to our project for parallel finite element scenario runs.

The third suggestion was to put in an extra hour a day to complete all the tasks before the design review.

The fourth suggestion was to deliver the structural interface drawings in four weeks to our customer. I had to ask our customer's project manager to commit to review and approve structural interface drawings in two weeks by the design review meeting date.

All these suggestions came from my team members. Nothing was forced down their throats. They all had a can-do attitude. I issued the meeting minutes in a controlled fashion through our document control and made sure that the company president got a copy.

After the meeting I went to the manufacturing department manager's office and explained the situation. I asked him to assign a particular engineer as a checker to my team for six weeks. I also mentioned to him that checking by his senior manufacturing engineer would benefit him later too in his manufacturing processes. His senior engineer would catch early all the missing critical dimensions and tolerances in the drawings for manufacturing. He was very kind and he accepted my request. He had no other choice. If he refused, my next step was to bring the company president into the picture.

My next stop was to the IT department manager's office. I asked him for two more workstations for six months, which he did not have laying around in the company. We agreed to lease them for six months and get the expenses charged to my project.

Then I sent an e-mail to my customer's project manager to have a call with him at 6 a.m. in the morning my time and 4 p.m. his time in Helsinki, to discuss a change in the design review date. I wrote in my e-mail that we would like to pull in the design review date by two weeks. I also mentioned that if he was not available at my requested call time, he should specify a time that was convenient for him.

Around 10:30 p.m. that night, I checked my company e-mail from home and saw that I had received an answer from Helsinki. My counterpart at the customer informed me that he would be ready for my phone call at 4 p.m. his time. I set my clock to 5 a.m. and went to bed anticipating a long day in front of me.

The next day, I called my customer's project manager at 6 a.m. my time. After initial greetings I explained to him that I had excess manpower in my project and things were looking ahead of schedule. I would like to transmit to him the structural interface drawings in four weeks and asked him to review them and approve them in two weeks after receipt. He did not see any problems with that. Then I explained to him that we would be able to complete all the design calculations and drawings in six weeks for the design review. Could he and his colleagues come to our facilities two weeks earlier for the design review meeting? He said he would discuss the new design review meeting date with his two colleagues and inform me in 24 hours by e-mail if they could make it.

Next, I brought up the phase 1 payment issue. I told him if all goes well during the design review meeting could he also pull in the phase 1 payment by two weeks. He said he had to discuss that with their financial and purchasing people and also get back to me. I emphasized that this payment was important to my company's cash flow and asked him to do his best to make it happen. He promised that he would do his best to pull in the phase 1 payment. Then I got an e-mail from him that evening informing me that he and two of his colleagues could make it to our facilities two weeks earlier at the specified new design review date. He was also working on the phase 1 early payment issue.

I called the next day to thank him for accepting the earlier design review, and found him at his desk. I told him that I would make the hotel arrangements close to our facilities at the company rate and we would also provide them with a company car. These small gestures were very much appreciated by him. He told me that he was still working on the phase 1 early payment issue. He estimated that he would have a final answer to me in a week.

I documented the highlights of my calls to the customer's contract manager and released them in document control and made sure the company president got a copy. Next I made an appointment with the company president, as I had promised in three days, and explained to him the status of the two week pull-in of my project. I told him that the condensed time schedule was doable with the added resources and equipment. I also emphasized all the cost overruns that had to be absorbed. Our customer's review team could make it to the design review meeting at the new specified time. The only open issue was early payment by our customer for phase 1. I told him that the customer's project manager was working on this issue diligently and would have an answer to us in a week. I asked my company president not to disturb the boat and go to higher-ups in our customer's company for this early payment issue. I was more than optimistic that the customer's project manager would come through after dealing with their inner procedures and politics.

My team's work stress level went up a couple of notches for the next six weeks. The customer's project manager came back with good news in a week that they would be able to pay us two weeks earlier, if we met all the phase 1 requirements. All of us, especially our company president, were very happy to hear this news from our customer. We all worked hard to make the condensed project schedule. We sent out the released structural interface drawings to our customer in four weeks. These drawings were approved by them before the design review meeting. We had our internal design review a week earlier than the formal one. We made sure that our design conformed to all customer specifications. After some minor modifications we were ready for our customer except the control panel software code.

The control panel software code was similar to an earlier one we designed for another customer. The code needed several modifications, but my team's electrical engineer would not have enough time to complete, test, and release it in time for the design review meeting. We decided to present the earlier version of the code and the required modifications to the customer. We were going to propose to the customer releasing the code in two weeks after the design review. This would not have affected any of the manufacturing processes, which were the next phase of the project.

The two-day design review meeting with the customer went well. We had the meetings start at 8 a.m. in the morning and conclude at 2 p.m. in the afternoon considering our guests' jet-lagged condition. I did not forget to put the U.S. and Finnish flags in the middle of the conference table. We had lunch brought in during the meetings. We provided our guests with private offices with Internet connections, printers, and phones as they needed. The customer's review team was very understanding to grant us a waiver from phase 1 deliverables and a two-week extension for the release of the control panel software code. Overall the design review meetings went well. We accepted all of the minor modifications the customer requested. Toward the end of the meeting, I arranged for our company president to come into the conference room and give a short appreciation and thank you talk to our customer's team and to my team.

At the end of the second day, I provided our customer's team with the released meeting minutes and action items list. Afterward, the customer's team and my whole team went out to a Mexican dinner to celebrate the achievement of a crucial milestone in our project two weeks early. Our Finnish guests enjoyed different flavored quesadillas and margaritas. The customer's team left town with great satisfaction. Our company president was very happy. I was very proud of my project team.

LESSONS LEARNED FROM THIS PROJECT EVENT

- Your company's financial stability can change suddenly and can affect your ongoing project unexpectedly.
- How to change your project goals in a team environment.
- How to approach your customer for an unusual request.
- Utilizing other company resources efficiently when you are in a bind.

Case 1.2: Protecting Intellectual Property during a Technology Transfer to a Japanese Company

My computer component company made a financial agreement with a Japanese company. As a result of this agreement we had to develop and transfer an advanced magnetic recording head technology along with its wafer manufacturing processes to them. I was assigned as the project manager for this intellectual property transfer to Japan. The Japanese company decided to send, as part of the agreement, to our wafer factory in California four Japanese engineers for a year to learn all details of wafer processes and our design specifications for intellectual property transfer.

I had to get ready for my guests in four weeks. They were going to come to the United States with their families. First, I arranged for them to stay in our company apartments, which were within walking distance to our factory. Second, I had to be very careful about the intellectual property transfer. We had many customers' products going through our production facilities. Every one of our customers was a fierce competitor of this Japanese company. We were only transferring a portion of my company's intellectual property to them. I had to set up guidelines for restricted areas in our plant. I had to confine these four engineers to certain sections of our plant. I had to identify the people that they could talk to or ask questions of. I had to make sure that they did not cross paths with our other customers when our other customers were visiting us. While preparing all the restrictions and precautions, I had to make sure that I was not violating any parts of the agreement between my company and the Japanese company.

Most importantly, I had to train all of the 3,000 people in our plant as to what to do and what to say when they encountered these Japanese engineers.

I had to move some of our engineers and create an isolated working space with four cubicles and a conference room for my Japanese guests. I also moved my office into this isolated section.

We had special telephone and Internet connections for them that were separate from the company ones. Japanese engineers could come to work from 8 a.m. to 5 p.m., Monday through Friday. They could not enter the plant during the swing and night shifts and during the weekends. If they had an inquiry or a question, they had to ask me first. I had to connect them with the right people from my company for the answers.

Training of my people was the hardest. I had to do the training in all shifts. I prepared a PowerPoint presentation that lasted 20 minutes. I presented the highlights of our agreement with the Japanese customer. I presented the names and the titles of the Japanese engineers that were visiting us. I outlined the isolated working space for them and when they were supposed to be in our plant. I detailed the do's and don'ts to protect our company's intellectual property. We were not to discuss anything except the advanced magnetic recording head technology along with its wafer manufacturing processes that was in our agreement. We were not to discuss with them any of our other customers and their products. We were not to discuss with them any of our other advanced magnetic recording head technologies.

The most crucial part of my training presentation was about the interface rules. I had to bring the Japanese engineer(s) with their questions to a particular person in our factory. Especially in our clean room wafer fabrication processes and in testing these interface rules were important. I did not want the Japanese engineers to observe our other proprietary processes. I trained everyone in our plant in four weeks including our president and our vice presidents.

The Japanese engineers came with their families and spent a very productive year with us. They obeyed all the rules and regulations I outlined for them. My company people were also very cautious and obedient to our intellectual property protection guidelines. I took them out to long sushi lunches and town tours when we had an important customer visit to our plant. I did not want to take the chance of them running into each other.

I became very good friends with these Japanese engineers. They taught me one Japanese word every day. So I learned close to 250 Japanese words and expressions from them. I invited them with their families to barbecue dinners at my house. I kept in touch with them many years after we all went our own ways in our lives.

Detailed preparations and training of my people for my company's intellectual property transfer to this Japanese company were the key elements for success. Even the Japanese company executives praised my project management guidelines to my superiors. They were very kind to send me a stainless steel water cooler as an appreciation gift for the work I did with their team.

LESSONS LEARNED FROM THIS PROJECT EVENT

- Intellectual property transfer within certain agreed upon boundaries can be very tricky between two companies.
- When a competitor's engineers visit your company for intellectual property transfer, the whole plant has to be ready to protect your technology.
- Interaction rules and guidelines with a competitor's engineers have to be fully detailed and explained to everyone in your company.
- Respect and good treatment of your competitor's engineers always pays off in the long run.

Case 1.3: Corporate Division Shutdown

I was a project manager for a data communication chip design company during the dot-com boom and bust periods. The dot-com bubble grew due to speculative investing for Internet-based companies, but these companies failed to turn a profit in a timely fashion. From 2000 to 2002, the Nasdaq Index lost about 80% of its value due to a rapid burst in the dot-com bubble. One day in 2001 we got the bad news that our corporate was going to close down our company's operations. I was right in the middle of a data communication chip design project. My customer was U.S. based. I had a group of five engineers working on my team. We all got very excited. The rumor mill was circulating at a very fast pace. My team's work efficiency immediately dropped. Everyone started to worry about his or her future rather than focusing on their tasks.

This chaotic situation lasted about 10 days. Then a group of executives from corporate came to our facilities and they finalized the details of our company's shutdown with our president. They gathered us in a large conference room and explained to us how the company shutdown was going to take place. It was a phase-out process. The first week they laid off 50% of the total workforce. They gave everyone a compensation package consisting of outstanding vacation pay and bonuses depending on seniority and salary level. Then they decided to phase out every project's remaining tasks. My project had another three months to go. A junior engineer from my team was laid off during the first week of the phase-out plan. I had four engineers and me to complete the project in three months.

I gathered my team and went over the remaining tasks one by one. If we worked efficiently without any glitches we were hopeful to complete the remaining project tasks in three months. I told my team members that they could spend a reasonable amount of time during the day to look for their future jobs. I emphasized that I would allow them to go to interviews during the week as long as they made up the lost time during off hours. We also decided that I was going to deal with our customer's project manager during these three months so that my team members did not get distracted and lose any precious time.

Then I called my customer's project manager and gave him the bad news about our company's closure. I assured him that his project was going to be completed in three months with a final acceptance review meeting before my team members and I left the company. I skipped the news about my junior engineer's early departure from my team. My customer's project manager had high confidence in me because I always delivered my commitments on time and with highest quality to him.

My team and I worked very closely during those final three months. Our offices were like a ghost town. All the cubicles were emptied out. During the phase-out process, we were saying goodbyes to several colleagues every week. I had lunch with my team members daily during those three months. During lunch we only discussed everyone's future plans. We never discussed the project tasks. We became a very close-knit bunch during those 13 weeks. I wrote outstanding recommendations for all my team members. We had to work a couple of weekends to complete all the remaining tasks. During the final week we had our internal acceptance review meeting. There were a couple of tasks that needed to be polished and retested. We had to extend our project one more week for the customer's final acceptance review.

I discussed my project's status with the company president. I told him that we needed an extra week to complete the project. He told me that he did not have any funds to cover my team's expenses for an extra week. During our team luncheon, I discussed the bind we were in with my team members. We all agreed to work another week without any compensation and complete the job. I immediately called my customer's project manager and explained our situation. I told him that we would be ready the following week for the final acceptance review. I told him that my team and I were working pro bono for a week to complete the project. He was very appreciative of our sacrifices.

The project's final acceptance review went without a hitch. Our customer accepted the data communication chip design without any change request. Afterward our customer's project manager took my team and me out to dinner to celebrate. Working as a very close-knit team during these hard times paid off well. We completed our project in 14 weeks. We came out of the dot-com bust with flying colors. My team members and I found jobs at other companies and immediately switched over to our new positions.

LESSONS LEARNED FROM THIS PROJECT EVENT

- Downsizing and/or shutting down a division of a corporation is very painful.
- Keeping up your project team's morale during difficult times is a challenge.
- A close-knit project team can overcome tough hurdles in chaotic times.
- Your customer always comes first.

Case 1.4: Airline Travel Fares Increased

I was the project manager to set up a volume production factory in Malaysia for our U.S.-based corporation. I had a team of design, manufacturing, quality, and test engineers in the United States and their counterparts in Malaysia. My engineers continually traveled back and forth from the United States to Malaysia to train and help the Malaysian engineers during the start-up period. During the initial months of the project, airline fares were very reasonable and I allowed my engineers to travel business class to Malaysia during their long 18-hour flight. Business class air travel gave them a fresh start at their destinations. They had a minimum amount of jet lag. They also accumulated a lot of airline miles for their personal use. My travel budget was about $200,000 per year. My travel budget allowed me to send about 40 engineers per year to Malaysia. I also brought several Malaysian engineers to the United States for training. We formed a kind of air corridor between our headquarters in the United States and our plant in

Malaysia. We had an in-house travel agent who took care of our travel needs. All of a sudden due to uncontrollable world events, the price of jet fuel started to increase. Airlines started to add surcharges on airfares. I started to overrun my travel budget.

My airline travel budget was going to almost double. I had to do something. I could not cut the number of trips made to Malaysia. The Malaysians needed hand holding and advice during the critical start-up period. I had a long meeting with my team. After several strong objections, I made them agree to fly in economy class. They were free to upgrade to business class with their own miles. It was not easy for my team members to buy into flying economy class for 18 hours. There were several other good suggestions made during our meeting. We agreed to fly during weekdays and to avoid holiday times such as Thanksgiving, Christmas, New Year, and spring breaks. One engineer suggested that our company's travel agent should secure a set of airline open tickets from airline promotions and sales events. We would use these open tickets when needed. I took on the assignment of negotiating the open ticket suggestion with our company's travel agent. Another suggestion was to station some of my team's engineers in Malaysia for a longer period of time instead of shuttling them back and forth every two or three weeks. Another suggestion was to increase and to emphasize videoconferencing meetings with our counterparts in Malaysia. I tried to implement all these suggestions. Most of these suggestions did not apply during emergency assignments. During an emergency situation, my engineers or me hopped on a plane immediately and flew to Malaysia. These were the budget breaking trips. The airline fares for these emergency trips were doubled or tripled. We had several of these emergency trips every year.

When I started the Malaysian project, fuel costs were about 10% of the airline operating costs. In two years, fuel costs edged up to about 35% of the airline operating costs. Airlines were passing on these operational cost increases to their customers. Air travel cost increases was reflected not only in ticket fares, but also in luggage fees, extra leg room fees, and so on. I went several times to my upper management to ask for an increase in my travel budget. I explained to them the steps we were taking to lower our travel expenses. I pleaded with them for a travel budget increase. Every time I was rejected. They emphasized that I should cut down on travel and keep my travel budget as it was.

With all the cautionary steps we took, I was still over my travel budget at the end of the project. When I presented my final cost performance report to my upper management, I separated the travel expenses budget from the rest of my project budget. My cost performance index for the travel budget was well below one. However, my cost performance index for the project budget, excluding the travel budget, was a little over one. My team and I did okay in our project's cost and schedule performances, except the travel cost dilemma. In the end, my upper management was very sympathetic about my travel budget cost overrun. They appreciated all the precautions we took to keep the travel costs down.

LESSONS LEARNED FROM THIS PROJECT EVENT

- A project's budget can be easily overrun by unexpected events.
- A team discussion to solve a nagging project issue always brings about good solutions.
- Detailed and logical project budget presentations to upper management can turn things around in your favor.

Case 1.5: Quality Assurance (QA) Department Undergoing a Major Overhaul

My project teams consisted of members from different departments in the organization. Every member reported to their particular department's manager and reported to me on a dotted line basis. I had no control of their performance reviews, promotions, salary increases, training, and personal issues. I always tried to help them in these areas. I made sure that their managers got my fair assessment and evaluation input in these areas in a timely fashion. In my reviews of each team member, I covered team play, customer relations, integrity, quality of work, reliability, stress management, ambition, attitude, attendance, communication skills, knowledge, and training and improvement needs.

During the manufacturing phase of an advanced safety vehicle project, I had two quality engineers on my team. They were responsible for receiving inspection of raw materials and subcomponents for the vehicle, for inspection of every weld on the vehicle, and inspection of every critical parameter on the vehicle. One day I came to work and learned that the manager of the quality department was let go due to some disagreements with the upper management. That same day, I learned that two quality engineers on my team who reported to the departed manager also gave notice and quit by taking their two-week vacations. The departed manager and two quality engineers had a very good and loyal camaraderie. I was suddenly without two quality engineers. I had to fill the quality engineering gap fast because the manufacturing of 10 vehicles was proceeding in full swing.

I went and discussed the quality engineering issue with my management and my human resources group. One remaining quality engineer was transferred to another group and she was not available for my project. She was fresh out of college and she did not have any experience in welding inspections. Our whole quality department was gone in a flash. I had to go outside and find other help in quality engineering. Hiring good engineers always took time. Finding experienced engineers was more time consuming. My only option was to go the consultant's way. My human resources department and I started to screen quality engineering consultants. We found a good consulting firm which was 120 miles away from our manufacturing operations. We interviewed them and agreed on hourly rates. My expenses for two consulting quality engineers were going to double. I had to get the okay from my management for an emergency budget increase. I called a quick meeting with my management and outlined the cost of the two consultants to my project. I explained to my management all the tasks the two quality engineers did for my project. Two quality engineers put in 50 to 60 hours each a week to complete my project's quality requirements. After an hour of bickering about signing up only one consultant instead of two, my management gave in and agreed with my two consultants' proposal. Our human resources and purchasing departments came together and signed a contract with the consulting firm in two days. The consulting firm assigned two of their senior quality engineers to my project. The consulting engineers stayed in a motel close to our facilities on our nickel during the week. They each put in 40 hours per week. My quality engineering budget went up by almost 100% during the next nine months.

I also had to micromanage both consultants. I had to indoctrinate them to our way of reporting and to our customer's contract requirements. They got acclimated fast and contributed heavily to my project.

It took my management one year to set up a new and stable quality department from scratch. I had to do whatever it took to complete my project's manufacturing phase on time within my customer's specifications.

LESSONS LEARNED FROM THIS PROJECT EVENT

- As project managers, we have to live peacefully and effectively with our team members who are not our direct reports.
- Unexpected events can happen in all company departments during the execution of your project, which are beyond your control.
- You have to stand your ground with your upper management in order to get the best solution for your project.

Case 1.6: Internal Project Direction

Disk drive magnetic head assemblies needed very precise alignment of their components. In volume production alignment of components was being performed by skilled operators under high-powered microscopes using precision tooling. Skilled labor costs were increasing and the sale price of the magnetic head assemblies was decreasing. It was a very competitive and fast-paced industry. The only way to get around the skyrocketing labor cost issue in the United States forced my company to move our magnetic head assembly operations to South Korea and to Malaysia. To set up offshore operations was a tough decision by our board of directors. The motto in the computer industry in the 1980s was to emigrate or to evaporate.

My company was very successful in their operations in South Korea and in Malaysia. I was heavily involved in setting up our Malaysian plant's operations. I lived there for six months to monitor, spearhead, and train our new Malaysian engineering group. However, at the same time the magnetic recording heads were getting smaller and component alignment requirements were getting tighter and tighter. Our alignment process capabilities were coming to a limit with skilled operators under high-powered microscopes using precision tooling.

The next step was to implement assembly processes using automation. Handling of small components delicately and aligning them to specifications of 0.0001 of an inch in volume production could be done by microrobots in an automated assembly module. This was a new concept for our volume production assembly lines. We were going to load components at one end of the automated assembly module and unload an assembled magnetic head at the other end. If successful, we could reduce our assembly labor force quite a bit and tighten our alignment process capability by twofold. Also an automated assembly module would give us a very favorable edge in the eyes of our customers. The executive vice president of engineering in our company was in favor of this futuristic automated assembly system, but the initial project cost was a major hurdle. Therefore, the company president and our board were against it.

There was another group of manufacturing engineers in our company who favored a semiautomated approach to our alignment processes. In this approach, a microrobot was going to handle the components, but again a skilled operator was going to perform the alignment operation under a high-powered microscope. This semiautomated alignment process was cheaper to implement, but it did not reduce our assembly labor force and it did not improve our alignment process capability. This semiautomated alignment process improved our throughput and reduced the amount of damaged components.

The executive vice president of engineering gave me the task of putting together an extensive feasibility study in three months in order to give direction to our magnetic head manufacturing processes for the next generation of our products. I chose two senior manufacturing engineers for my feasibility study team. First, three of us put together detailed system specifications for an automated assembly module and for a semiautomated assembly module. An important characteristic of both types of modules was flexibility and programmability from one product to another in a short time. Then we sourced three potential automation houses in the United States that were experienced in handling delicate micro components with robots. We visited them several times and received bids from them per our specifications. We chose an automation house in the Boston area as the leading candidate, if our board of directors would approve along with the automated or semiautomated assembly project.

We compared three different assembly systems with their advantages, disadvantages, and investment payback periods in three different countries, namely, the United States, Malaysia, and South Korea. We performed sensitivity analyses to risk factors such as project delays, personnel training, and spare parts. The whole feasibility report ended up being close to 300 pages. Then we prepared a five-page executive summary for the whole report. The report had to go through several review phases before being presented to our board of directors. We first presented the report to our manufacturing managers in the United States, Malaysia, and South Korea. Then we made a presentation to the group of manufacturing engineers in our company who favored a semiautomated approach to our alignment processes. All of them had constructive criticism and good input to improve our feasibility report. We modified our report accordingly and made our final presentation to our executive vice president of engineering. He liked the report as it was and praised our very detailed and methodical approach and timely completion of the project. He told us to be ready to present it to our board of directors during the board's next meeting.

I made a half-hour presentation to my company's board of directors about three assembly options in three countries that we studied. The manual assembly line in the United States was our baseline for comparative analyses. Board members were only interested in investments' payback periods and their effects on our cash flow projections. They did not ask one question regarding technical aspects of the automated and the semiautomated projects. I was amazed. At the end of the meeting, we got the automated assembly project approved unanimously for our Malaysian plant. Our executive vice president of engineering was very happy with the result. He took my team out to lunch and congratulated me and my team members for a job well done.

Internal projects in a company can have very competitive directions. To find the right project direction for the company might require a detailed prestudy. I have experienced several projects ending up on the shelf and costing bundles because of rushed and personally favored executive decisions.

LESSONS LEARNED FROM THIS PROJECT EVENT

- There are several different ways to approach improvement projects for the future of a company.
- There are always conflicting views and passions for improvement projects within a company.
- Decisions for a company's future projects should be made by relying on sound data and good analysis instead of shooting from the hip.

Case 1.7: Upper Management Stability during a Project

Stability in the upper management of a company affects smooth progress of a project tremendously. Personnel and responsibility changes in upper management during the execution of a project can cause ripple effects and sometimes tsunami effects to your project. It is possible to shield your project from these effects to a certain extent, but in most cases your project gets hurt too.

A challenging case of upper management shuffle occurred during the execution of an internal product development project that was under my direction. During the execution phase of my development project, the board of directors of our company fired our president and brought in a new one who was hijacked from a well-respected technology company. The new president brought in a dozen of his colleagues from the computer industry in order to pursue his vision of our company. Some of the new arrivals were positioned into upper management, especially into the engineering divisions. Others were positioned into the research and development group. Two new senior scientists joined my product development group. These scientists were good buddies with the new president. They had worked together more than a decade.

I presented my project's mission, team, and status to the new management. They all had numerous inputs to my project's mission and schedule. They completely changed the direction of my project with new target completion dates. My project was turned topsy-turvy by the new upper management. All the changes were approved by the new president without any hesitation. He had complete confidence in his new upper management team. I had six engineers working for me on my team. With the addition of two senior scientists, my team expanded to eight people. All of a sudden the morale of my six engineers went downhill. Everything we had done for a year before these changes occurred was thrown out the window.

First, I had a team meeting with the old engineers on my team. We discussed what we had accomplished and what we had to do under the new upper management direction. I had to convince them one by one that we did very well in our product development. The new product development direction was not their failure, but it was a new outlook for the future of our company and to our competition. Also, I emphasized that we had to be open-minded and welcome two new members of our team and make them feel at home in their new environment.

As a project manager I had to start a brand new project with a new mission and new deadlines. On top of it all, I had to blend the two new senior scientists into my team and make sure that there were no animosities between the old-timers and the newcomers. I had to accept all proposed changes to my project. These were the new bosses. We could not continue with our old ways. We had to go along with the new leaders. I had an extended team meeting to brainstorm our new project, to discuss new tasks and team members' responsibilities. During the meeting, I had to carefully bring the two new senior scientists into our team atmosphere. I had to make them realize that I was the team leader and they had to execute tasks that were assigned to them by me in a time frame that was on our schedule. Most importantly they had to coordinate with other team members very closely. They were good buddies with our new president, but they had to realize that their first priority was my project.

The new project started well. After a couple of weeks, the two new senior scientists on my team started to deviate from their task objectives and specifications without notifying me. Evidently, they were being redirected by our new president. These ripples also affected my other six team members and they started complaining to me about sudden changes in the project's direction. I had to correct this disharmonious situation immediately. I made an appointment directly with the new president and explained to him politely the issues I was having in managing my new product development project effectively. He apparently was going out to lunch weekly with the two new senior engineers on my team. They were discussing the status of my project and he was making some suggestions on the spot without realizing his suggestions' effects on the whole execution of the project. We finally agreed that if he had any new suggestions regarding my project, he would e-mail me first. After my assessment of the impact of his suggestions on my project's schedule and cost, I would inform him the consequences before making a final decision to my project's modified direction and specifications.

Upper management changes in a company can positively or negatively impact internal project directions, project teams, management styles, and project reporting styles. As project managers, we have to deal cleverly and in a timely manner with the changing world around us.

LESSONS LEARNED FROM THIS PROJECT EVENT

- Stability in your upper management helps in smooth sailing of your project.
- A change in the upper management of your company always brings new ideas and new management styles that can affect your project.

- As project managers, we have to mold our project team members into our new management's styles.
- As project managers, we have to have open minds in dealing with our new upper management's directives, which affect our projects.

Case 1.8: Help from the Legal Department

The legal department of a company can help a project manager a lot in detailing a project's contract agreement conditions. Some conditions might contradict each other. Others might be written in a very complicated legal language. Some conditions have to be renegotiated with the customer's legal department. A contract manager has to fully understand at the beginning of the project all contract agreement conditions for delays in deliveries, patents, copyrights, trademarks, force majeure, subcontracting rules, and governing laws and arbitration. In addition to understanding all contract agreement conditions, he has to relay them to his team members in layman's terms. The whole project team has to realize what happens if there is a delay in deliverables or if there is an invention during the execution of the project. If some of these contract agreement conditions are overlooked, they might come back to bite you during the execution of a project or at the end of the project and lead to irrecoverable damage to your company.

I had a very interesting case regarding delivery of final documents and drawings at the end of a project. I delivered my project's hardware on time, but I was delayed six weeks in delivering final documents and drawings to my customer. Delays in final documents and drawings deliveries were mainly caused by delays in my customer's timely approval of preliminary versions. Also, I lost two of my engineers to other projects during the winding down period of my project. My contract agreement specified a penalty of 0.1% of total contract value for each week of delay in delivery of final documents and drawings. Six weeks of delay added up to a handsome penalty to my company.

I discussed this delay issue with my customer's project manager on the phone every week. He told me not to worry about the penalty clause regarding delivery of final documents and drawings. He knew that his team's delays in their responses were a major part of the blame. I delivered all final deliverables six weeks late and the project came to a close. More than a month passed and I got a call from our chief financial officer. He told me that my company was being penalized 0.6% of total contract value due to delays in delivering final documents and drawings to my customer. This was quite a shock to me. I explained the final documents and drawings delivery issues to our chief financial officer. I emphasized the lackadaisical comments of my customer's project manager. I told him that I had all of the recorded delivery dates to our customer for every document and drawing. I also had all of the receipt dates and comments from our customer to me for every document and drawing. We agreed that we should not be penalized for this delay. We had every right to appeal the penalty.

Then we called my customer's project manager to understand the reasons behind the penalty. My customer's project manager insisted that he had nothing to do with the penalty. Higher-ups in his company decided to apply the penalty clause because of the six-week delay in delivering final documents and drawings. My customer's project manager apologized for misleading me and he stressed that he could do nothing to reverse the penalty.

Then our chief financial officer and I agreed to bring our legal department into the picture to pursue our rightful case. Our lawyers talked to their lawyers. Our presidents were also involved as they too discussed the penalty case. My customer was not budging regarding the penalty at all. We decided to take the case to the next level, namely to arbitration, because of the stiffness of the penalty and because we felt that we had the upper hand to win the case. According to the contract agreement conditions, disputes between parties arising in connection with or related to my project had to be settled by final and binding arbitration under the rules of arbitration of the International Chamber of Commerce in Helsinki, Finland. Thankfully, the arbitration language was English.

I briefed one of our lawyers with all details of the case. I provided him with all recorded delivery and receipt dates of documents and drawings. Our lawyer applied for the arbitration. He had to go to Helsinki for the hearing. After a full day of arbitration sessions, the arbitrators decided to drop the penalty. Later our lawyer told me that the reason we won the case was due to my detailed delivery and receipt dates of documents and drawings. I made the mistake of not getting the "nothing to worry about the penalty clause" comments in writing from my customer's project manager. Our legal department came to my rescue. I was very appreciative of our legal department's efforts. We celebrated our victory over a nice dinner when our lawyer got back from Helsinki.

LESSONS LEARNED FROM THIS PROJECT EVENT

- A company's legal department is a crucial advisor and a lifesaver to a project manager.
- Some conflicts between you and your customer or between you and your subcontractors have to be resolved with the help of your legal department.
- Keeping accurate records of communication and of deliveries between you and your customer and between you and your subcontractors is a must.
- In a project execution, verbal promises and directives are worthless.

Case 1.9: Salary and Compensation Variations in a Global Team Environment

I did engineering, engineering management, and engineering project management for over 46 years. I loved my engineering challenges. I stayed in my field and did not regret a bit in choosing this very fulfilling field early on in my life. The majority of my engineering colleagues were also satisfied with their career choices. Despite long work hours, every engineer I knew wanted to grow and wanted to be challenged in his or her work. This was the engineering environment that I experienced in the United States. As I got to know and to work with engineers from other countries, professional satisfaction levels degraded quite a bit. The motivation levels of engineers dropped due to lower salary and compensation packages in other countries. For example, engineers in Europe and in Japan are compensated about 70% of what U.S. engineers get. Salary and compensation packages get worse, about 20% of those in the United States, in countries like Malaysia, India, and China. As engineering project teams and workforces get more and more integrated globally, engineering salary and compensation packages are ratcheting up in developing countries.

When Malaysian engineers were part of my volume production setup team, I always reminded my U.S. engineers not to discuss salaries, compensation packages, raises, or bonuses with their Malaysian counterparts. Money issues were very touchy subjects in a global project environment. I made many recommendations for salary increases and for bonuses to the supervisors of Malaysian engineers who were on my team without any success. The main mission of our Malaysian operation's general manager and Malaysian supervisors was to keep costs down. They did not value engineering qualifications, experience, and work ethics like we do in the United States. They were also leaving most engineering positions unfilled in order to keep costs down and thereby squeezing long work hours from their engineering staff. There was a substantial amount of turnover in my Malaysian engineering workforce. I could not keep a stable engineering environment in my Malaysian project teams.

I lost a couple of Malaysian engineers right in the middle of a project due to salary increase disputes. I got them well trained at the beginning of the project. They were in the process of becoming very qualified in their tasks and they were smart and hard workers. They learned somehow that their counterparts in the United States got 10% increases in annual salary reviews and they got nothing. They confided in me that they were ready to leave our company because of unfair annual salary increase and bonus distribution practices in our Malaysian subsidiary. I pleaded with their supervisor and with our Malaysian general manager to stop those two Malaysian engineers from leaving our company. The Malaysian managers' attitude was that there were many unemployed engineers out there and they could hire them at a much lower salary. Due to the Malaysian managers' stubbornness and short-sightedness, I wasted all the training time for those two engineers and several of my project's tasks were set back by two weeks.

Salary and bonus discontent among engineers is increasing in developing countries. Engineers in these countries are less satisfied with their engineering careers and they are ready to jump ship and/or change careers in order to improve their lives.

At the other end of the global engineering workforce spectrum, there are countries like South Korea and Singapore where engineering is well respected and well appreciated and therefore well rewarded. In an internal project team, I had several engineers from our South Korean subsidiary who were working for me. They also had unequal pay, about 50% in the 1990s, for equal work as compared to their U.S. counterparts. Their supervisors and our general manager in South Korea were more willing to go along with my annual salary increases and bonus distributions recommendations. They valued an engineer's training, qualifications, and experience. As South Korea improved their economy at lightning speed, their engineering salaries and bonuses climbed up to about 70% in the 2000s as compared to their U.S. counterparts. I think a significant portion of South Korea's economic success was due to their well-satisfied, well-appreciated, and hard working engineering workforce. I had similar good experiences with Singaporean engineers on my project teams. They were very happy and very satisfied with their careers.

I believe that salary and compensation discussions in a global team environment should be taboo. As global project managers, we have to sensitize our team members not to discuss money matters with our colleagues from other countries.

LESSONS LEARNED FROM THIS PROJECT EVENT

- In an international project team environment, work motivation levels alter quite a bit from country to country.
- You have to advise your U.S.-based engineers not to discuss their compensation packages with engineers in other countries.

Case 1.10: Lessons Learned from Previous Projects

Historical knowledge of projects completed in a company is a very valuable guide for a global project manager. In particular, lessons learned from historical projects can shed light and show the right path to avoid making the same mistake over and over again. As project managers, during execution of a global project, we always run into issues with specifications, schedules, budgets, team members, company upper management, customers, regulatory agencies, foreign governments, subcontractors, inspectors, suppliers, and so on. As we get ready to close out a project, we should compile all the lessons learned from that project along with actions taken and results achieved in a report. We should release this report in document control. We should also present pertinent sections of this report to our team members, to our upper management, to our customers, and to our subcontractors.

The lessons learned report for a completed project was a requirement for a company that I worked for. Reviewing these reports about a customer's previous projects gave me a very good understanding of what I should be prepared for in dealing with this particular customer. In particular, my customer's unannounced audits of man-hours and materials charged to my project surprised me a lot. My customer's auditors came to our company unannounced and reviewed our charge records for every one of their previous projects. As a project manager I had never experienced unannounced auditor visits before. We had had several issues with this company with incorrect charges in the past. So I started to check our charge records every two weeks and made the necessary corrections with our accounting department. I was audited unannounced twice by my customer's auditors during the execution of my project for man-hours and material charges. They found everything in order and our accounting department and I received good pats on the back.

In another offshore oil platform equipment design project, pollution control laws, ordinances, rules, and regulations were very detailed and complicated. Pollution control involved several government agencies such as the U.S. Department of the Interior, U.S. Geological Survey, U.S. Army Corps of Engineers, and the U.S. Coast Guard. I reviewed my company's historical documents related to similar past projects and discussed pollution control procedures with seasoned engineers who worked on previous similar projects. I formulated a very thorough plan to prevent pollution during the execution of my project. I trained my team members as to what to do in case of undesirable and uncontrolled spills and leaks. Every member of my team was very diligent in pollution prevention while performing his or her task.

Another useful lesson that I learned was in dealing with material safety data sheets for chemicals that were used in one of my projects. My customer paid lots of attention to material safety data sheets for all chemicals used in my project. From historical information, I prepared a list of laboratories certified by my customer that could issue material safety data sheets. I put together a data sheet form that was acceptable to my customer's project manager. In my project schedule, I included all dates for when I had to submit samples to certified laboratories and when material safety data sheets were due to my customer.

Lessons learned information was crucial for a customer's design review process. What had surprised us during design review meetings in the past? What kind of issues had we encountered during meetings? How did we deal with incomplete and missing information? Did we have any specification clarification issues? How did we deal with a customer's instantaneous add-ons to the project? One thing I learned was to take a time-out from the meeting or call for a break, if an unanswerable question or request popped up. Then I huddled with my team in private and we collectively decided on an answer in a calm environment before facing my customer with an answer.

In another lessons learned case, I found out that a particular final inspector always randomly checked torques of several bolts on equipment being inspected. I asked my manufacturing manager to go over and verify each bolt's torque on every piece of equipment that was ready for inspection before the inspector arrived. In the past, this final inspector also randomly checked paint thickness on every surface of the equipment. Also, in the past, there had been several issues with this final inspector not signing off our equipment, but at the end of my project we were ready for him. We inspected every piece of our equipment to be shipped just as he would have inspected it. We made a couple of touch-ups and corrections as needed. The final inspector was very surprised not to find any issues with our equipment during his final inspection. I was thankful for my company's lessons learned documents.

LESSONS LEARNED FROM THIS PROJECT EVENT

- Do not forget to release your "Lessons Learned" report in your document control during the closure phase of your project.
- Present "Lessons Learned" from your project to your team members, to your upper management, to your customers, and to your subcontractors before interest in your project fades away.

Case 1.11: The Effect of an Outside Consulting Firm on a Project

In most companies, upper management has a hard time making decisions. Officers of the company procrastinate a lot and put off important decision making. As project managers, these kinds of important decision delays can affect our projects and our performances. We can only write our warning e-mails, prepare our reports, and have urgent discussions with upper management with little effect on their decision-making process.

In such a case, I was assigned by our president to prepare a feasibility report to expand our production operations into Europe and into Southeast Asia. I was given six months to prepare a detailed report on expanding into certain countries like France and South Korea. I prepared a long list of questions for their foreign investment representatives. I visited all those countries and I learned in detail their investment incentives such as duty-free zone rules and requirements, investment loan conditions, foreign company taxation rules, labor and union laws, wages and salaries, and so on. I also got lots of help from international subsidiaries of an investment firm. I prepared a comparative feasibility study that detailed investment amounts by year and estimated returns on these investments. I outlined facility needs, equipment, and personnel requirements. I also listed all risk areas in utilities, in unions, in training, and so forth. I summarized my report in four pages for my upper management. I gave the full report with its summary to four executives in my company one week before the final delivery date.

Our president called a meeting with company executives about expansion of our production operations and asked me to present my feasibility report. All of the executives were focused on amounts and returns on the company's investment. Overall my presentation went well. They all praised my report.

Three months passed and there was no word on expansion. I asked several executives what was going on. They all replied that they were in the decision-making process with no definite date in sight. One day I received a call from my boss informing me that they had hired a consulting firm to perform a similar feasibility study to mine. The president and the board of directors wanted a second opinion before launching into a foreign expansion project. I was disappointed at my upper management's decision but I had to live with it.

Four representatives from the consulting firm came to our facilities and settled into four offices for three months. Every one of them interviewed me almost daily. They asked me hundreds of questions about our production equipment, about the countries I visited, about labor and engineer training requirements in those countries, and so on. I provided them with all the information they needed. They also received lots of input from their subsidiaries in France and in South Korea. The consulting firm completed their feasibility report in four months and presented it to my company's executives. I was not invited to the presentation meeting, but I did receive a copy of their report from my boss. The consulting firm's conclusions were very similar to mine. My company spent millions of dollars to get a second opinion from the consulting firm on the foreign expansion project. My company's executives and our board of directors needed that assurance from the consulting firm before taking a big step forward in the foreign expansion project. Finally, after a year and a half, they made a decision to go ahead with the project.

During my career I have seen all types of decision makers in company executives. Some were high-risk takers, while others were very conservative. High-risk takers made fast decisions which emerged from their gut feelings and from their experiences. Conservative executives took their time to make a decision. They consulted many people during the decision-making process. They would get several reports compiled about the subject. Some executives could not even make a decision by themselves and would opt for an executive group decision. In our fast-moving and very competitive business environment, cautious risk takers are the winners.

LESSONS LEARNED FROM THIS PROJECT EVENT

- Some upper management people procrastinate a lot and put off important decision making.
- Some upper management people need extra assurance from different and reliable sources before making important decisions.

Case 1.12: Japanese Customer Visit to Qualify Our South Korean Plant for Volume Production

As an American magnetic recording head manufacturing company, we were successful in getting qualified as a component supplier to a major Japanese disk drive manufacturer. One last hurdle in this relationship was to get our South Korean magnetic recording head manufacturing plants to be qualified by our Japanese customer. In my previous visits to our South Korean plants, I observed bitter antagonism toward the Japanese because of Japan's colonization of Korea during the first half of the 20th century. I was afraid that my engineering team in South Korea would not be able to control themselves during the qualification process and show their bitterness toward our Japanese customer.

In the beginning of the 20th century, Japan colonized Korea. Japan established economic and military dominance in Korea. Japanese rulers forced Koreans to adapt to Japanese cultural and religious practices. Koreans were forced to change their names to Japanese ones. Over 50% of arable land was turned over to the Japanese owners and many Korean landowners became tenant farmers overnight. All Korean newspapers were shut down. Korean children were only allowed to have a primary school education.

All factories were owned by the Japanese. Japanese rulers created a strict system of colonial mercantilism to exploit Korean raw materials and Korean manpower for their World War II efforts. After the Japanese surrender in 1945, the Soviet Union and the United States agreed to split the Korean peninsula at the 38th parallel (the demilitarized zone). The southern region of the peninsula became a democratic republic called the *Republic of Korea* and the northern region became a communist regime called the *Democratic People's Republic of Korea.*

In order to ease the tensions between my Korean engineering team and the visiting Japanese qualification team, I decided to go to Korea first for two weeks to prepare and to train my Korean team for our Japanese customer's qualification process both psychologically and technically.

I had meetings with my Korean engineering team daily. I told them that the historical relationship with Japan was bitter. However, South Korea was trying to advance technologically and catch up to Japan in standard of living. I emphasized South Korea's national ambitions and asked my team members to restrain themselves from showing their antagonistic feelings during the upcoming qualification. If our Japanese customer qualified our South Korean plant as a sole source component supplier for their automated disk drive assembly line that would be a great step forward for the South Korean economy. All the team members agreed and were upbeat about the qualification process.

We did three trial qualification runs. I acted as the Japanese customer during the trial runs. I bombarded them with questions and inquiries about critical parameters, process controls, and our historical capabilities at every manufacturing station. We reviewed and polished all our statistical process controls from receiving inspection, through every assembly process, to final shipment to customer. We reviewed our disposition procedures for out-of-specification situations. We reviewed our operator training and production line qualification methods. At the end of two weeks, my Korean team was ready for our Japanese customer.

During the introductory meeting, I took the floor and praised my Korean team and gave examples of their accomplishments in process and in quality control. Our Japanese customer gave us a list of items that they would like to investigate. We obliged them in every item that they requested. They toured our assembly line during the day shift and also during the night shift. They asked specific questions of the operators about their tasks. The qualification process lasted for four days. There were several minor glitches here and there, but my team worked very hard to correct them and found the right answers. My team was also very courteous during lunches and dinners with our guests.

At the end of the fourth day, the head of the Japanese delegation took the floor and praised our Korean operations. They found only one flaw in our clean room monitoring control charts. They wanted the temperature, humidity, and particle count monitored every half an hour instead of every two hours. We agreed to their request. Our Japanese customer qualified our South Korean plant as the sole source for their magnetic recording head assemblies. One month after the qualification, we started shipping from South Korea to Japan a high quantity of magnetic recording head assemblies directly to their automated disk drive manufacturing line in a kanban system.

After our Japanese customer left we had a team meeting. I thanked every member of my South Korean team for their outstanding efforts during the qualification process. That night I invited them out to dinner to celebrate their psychological and technical success. I do not remember how many bottles of soju were consumed during dinner. Since I do not drink I could not participate in their drinking ceremony from the same shot glass that went around the table.

LESSONS LEARNED FROM THIS PROJECT EVENT

- In a global project environment, learn the histories of the countries you are dealing with.
- Prepare your project team for sensitive issues between countries that might negatively affect your project.
- Always praise and recognize your project team after a successful project event.

Case 1.13: The Customer Placed a Permanent Observer in Our Plant and in Our Subcontractor's Plant

My company was chosen as the sole source custom component supplier to a large U.S. computer manufacturer. I had a team of engineers who worked only for the design and manufacturing of this custom component. We designed and developed the custom component in the United States and manufactured it in South

Korea. We also had several key subcontractors for this custom component in Japan. Our customer was very diligent regarding industrial espionage and protecting their intellectual property. They required us to apply very strict rules and regulations to protect their customized design and product details. In a fast developing and very competitive computer industry, intellectual property protection was top priority.

During the development and qualification of the custom component I had to relocate my project team to an isolated location in our U.S. facilities. They could not discuss the custom component with anyone else outside my team. The custom component's test facility was also separated from other test laboratories. The customer placed a resident engineer into my group to oversee all our activities and to make sure that their intellectual properties were fully protected. The custom component development and qualification went very well for three months with several minor glitches. Some engineers left several drawings on their desks at night, which was not acceptable. All drawings had to go into the vault at night. One engineer made a copy of a drawing without getting my and the resident engineer's permission. We were ready for offshore manufacturing. Our facilities in South Korea and our subcontractor in Japan had to be qualified for volume production and these facilities and the people working on this project had to be prepared for intellectual property protection.

Production areas for the custom component both at our subcontractor and at our facilities were separated by gray plastic walls. All engineers and other personnel working on this project were trained on intellectual property protection rules and guidelines. I traveled with the customer's team both to Japan and to South Korea to qualify them for intellectual property protection procedures. Everything went smoothly during the qualifying inspection and volume production started on time. The customer assigned a resident engineer to our plant in South Korea. This resident engineer also traveled to Japan to check on our subcontractor every fortnight.

After a month into volume production, the resident engineer got very sick from food poisoning in South Korea. He was taken to a hospital in the city of Chungju. I called my team's manager in South Korea and asked him to stay with the resident engineer all the time in the hospital. I asked my team's manager not to leave the sight of the resident engineer one minute until he got well. The resident engineer did not speak any Korean. Communication with the hospital personnel was a major issue. It was my responsibility to take care of him. My team's manager in South Korea stayed with him one week in the hospital. Apparently, the resident engineer lost lots of fluids during his food poisoning ordeal. He had to gain back his strength and his body fluids before being released from the hospital. He was very appreciative that we did not leave him alone in his struggle back to health. Even during his hospital stay, he reviewed and signed off on engineering change orders and on volume production out-of-specification lot dispositions.

The resident engineer stayed in our manufacturing facility in South Korea for a year without any other health issues. He did not even take a day of vacation during his stay in South Korea. He was very dedicated to his assignments. His supervisor and I went to South Korea to visit him several times during his stay there. His supervisor even gave the resident engineer's annual review to him in South Korea. His supervisor asked me to provide my input too regarding the resident engineer's performance in our U.S. facilities, in our South Korean facilities, and in our subcontractor's facilities. I provided him with very positive input about the resident engineer's performance at our and at our subcontractor's facilities.

The volume production of the custom component lasted for three years. My customer sent two more resident engineers to South Korea during this time. Their stay in South Korea went without any incident. At the end of the project, my customer was very appreciative of my team for taking good care of their resident engineers during their stay in South Korea and for doing a superb job in protecting their intellectual property.

LESSONS LEARNED FROM THIS PROJECT EVENT

- Protecting your customer's intellectual property during the execution of a project can require very detailed and careful planning.
- Customer's intellectual property protection is more difficult in foreign and competitive countries.

Case 1.14: Final Project Evaluation by the Customer

I was heading a data communication chip design project. We had the final design review. The chip design software was delivered to the customer. The customer built it and beta tested it successfully. I could never close out the project because the final project evaluation by the customer's project manager was missing. I needed a report card from my customer that identified my team's performance. My company and I wanted feedback that identified our good qualities, average qualities, and bad qualities during the execution of the project so that we could improve continually. Such a final project evaluation report covered evaluation of all team members, our design expertise, our test expertise, communication with the customer, on-time response, dealing with engineering change notices, and meeting their specification, schedule, and cost targets.

I nudged the customer's project manager for three months by e-mails and telephone calls after we delivered the final chip design software for the final project evaluation report. He was always apologetic that he did not have any time and that he had been given a new assignment to head a new large project for his company. I told him that I was onto a new project too, but I would very much like to close out his project. He felt that the project ended when we delivered the final version of the chip design software. He was not allocating any of his time for my final project evaluation report. So my project's final evaluation report was falling through the cracks. I did not want to go to his superiors and antagonize the guy. One day I heard from his secretary that he would be attending a chip design tools conference in San Francisco in two weeks.

I went to my manager's office and explained to him the situation about the stalled final evaluation report. I asked my manager if I could attend the conference in San Francisco to evaluate the advances in chip design tools for my company and also catch up with our customer's project manager to complete the final evaluation report on the spot. Since the project was completed three months ago, all of my project's charge numbers were closed. I was doing this extra work to complete the final project evaluation report on our overhead account. I told him what the cost of my three-day trip to the conference would be. My manager thought about my proposal for a couple of minutes. He said that he could finance my trip to the conference through his group's training account. I was very pleased to hear his approval of my trip. Finally, I was going to get a chance to close out my old project, which was hanging over my head like Damocles' sword.

I went to the conference. I was able to catch up with my customer's project manager during the first session. I told him about my persistent mission to finalize the project evaluation report. I assured him that I would not take more than half an hour of his time and I would ask the evaluation questions and I would jot down his answers. He only had to review the final report, sign, and date it. He finally agreed to get together with me for coffee the next morning. I was elated to see the light for the final project evaluation report at the end of the tunnel.

During the evening, I prepared all of the project evaluation questions that I was going to ask him. In our company, we had a standard final project evaluation form. I expanded on it. The next morning we met at Starbucks at the conference center. I treated him to a coffee of his choice. I went over every evaluation question one by one, got the response of the customer's project manager, and jotted the summary of his response on the evaluation form. The whole process took a little over 45 minutes. He reviewed the summarized report, signed, and dated it. His evaluation of the project was very favorable. He had several concerns about my project team. He mentioned that my team was composed of too many novice engineers and not enough seasoned ones. He recommended that our project teams should be more balanced in experience for future projects. His second important criticism was about my company's high overhead costs. My company was losing its competitive edge with high overhead costs. He advised that we should lower our overhead costs at least by 20%, if we wanted to win other projects from his company. These were two very crucial inputs from my customer. I thanked him for his time and for his honest evaluation of our project. I assured him that I would take his recommendations to my company's president and correct them to win his next contract in chip design.

When I got back, I made an appointment with the company president and went over the final project evaluation report. He thanked me for working hard to obtain constructive input from our customer. He was aware of our company's high overhead costs. He assured me that steps were being taken to lower them. He promised to distribute his manpower experience more evenly for the future projects.

The final project evaluation report by the customer can be hard to get. Sometimes it can be a pain in the neck to obtain it for a project manager. If it is done face-to-face with the customer, you can get good and honest advice for improvement.

LESSONS LEARNED FROM THIS PROJECT EVENT

- During the closure phase of your project, do not forget to get the final project evaluation report from your customer's project manager.
- Final project evaluation reports always fall through cracks as your customer's project manager and you go on to new assignments.
- Do all you can to catch up with your customer's project manager in order to complete the final project evaluation report.
- Input and comments from your customer's project manager are very important guidelines for your future projects.

Case 1.15: Filtering Information

I was the project manager for supplying all the U.S. manufactured wafer fabrication equipment for a Japanese high technology company. One of the high-end pieces of equipment that my customer was sourcing in the United States was the ion milling machine. The subcontractor for ion milling machines was located in Virginia. My customer ordered four ion milling machines for their new wafer fabrication plant in Malaysia. I was heavily involved in putting together specifications and shipment and delivery requirements for the ion milling machines.

I visited the ion milling machine subcontractor several times during the course of the project with and without my Japanese customer's representatives joining me. The project was scheduled to complete in 10 months. I was on the phone five days a week with my subcontractor's project manager discussing the status of my project. I updated my Japanese customer's project manager weekly on the progress made on the construction of ion milling machines.

The ion milling machine subcontractor built the best ones in the world at that time. While they were building my four standard ion milling machines, they had a large order to build 20 advanced ion milling machines from a very important customer. Everything they were doing for their important customer in their plant was blocked inside temporary plastic walls so that no one else could see the advanced ion milling machines that were being built there. Whenever I chatted with their engineers about their advanced product, their engineers were mum on the details. They only mentioned that these advanced ion milling machines had a 10-nanometer accuracy of uniform material removal from the surface of a 6-inch wafer.

I had to manage the communication with my Japanese customer appropriately without getting them excited while keeping their trust and respect in me and in our subcontractor at the highest level. I did not report to my Japanese customer every little detail of the project. I gave them a weekly status summary of the project and a weekly updated project schedule. There were several ups and downs every day regarding the ion milling machines' construction. Most of the down issues were solved within at most two weeks. These minute details were between me and my subcontractor's project manager. Some delays crept into my project due to the subcontractor's priority to his large advanced ion milling machines order. I immediately hopped on a plane from California to Virginia and showed myself at the door of my subcontractor and solved the project delay issues and other nagging issues face-to-face with him. We always found a way to catch up to the schedule by authorizing some overtime or by finding an outside machine shop that could build a component faster. I had to keep my credibility with my customer intact. By monitoring my subcontractor very closely and by not disturbing my customer, we completed the project on time, but we ran 5% over budget due to several overtime authorizations. My customer was very happy with the results.

Another issue was with my customer. My customer's project manager insisted that we perform a long-term capability study on all ion milling machines before they left the subcontractor's facility. However, the contract specified a short-term capability study requirement for all four machines before delivery. A long-term capability study meant taking a lot more data while running the machines. This would have delayed the shipments by at least two weeks and cost my subcontractor an extra 160 man-hours of work. I emphasized to my customer's project manager what our contract specified. I convinced him that the long-term capability studies should be performed at his factory after receiving the ion milling machines. After several discussions, he finally agreed with me. I did not even mention this extra work request from our customer to my subcontractor. My subcontractor was overstretched with respect to manpower. I had to protect him from our customer's extra requirements.

Communicating filtered information is the backbone of a project's control structure. How much information to pass on and how much you want to disturb the cart are crucial factors during the life of a project. If every little detail regarding your project goes up to your chief executive officer or goes to your customer, you are mismanaging your project. You have to filter out the ripples in your communicated information. At the same time you have to realize what information and when to inform your higher-ups and/or your customer without any delay.

A similar kind of information filtering goes both ways. If you receive some negative information regarding your customer, do not immediately spill it to your team members. Your customer might be going bankrupt. They might be shutting down your project. They might be changing project specifications. First, absorb the information yourself. Validate the information, understand its details, and weigh effects of the information on your team members, and then announce it as needed.

A similar kind of information filtering should happen internally. If you hear from your boss that a layoff is going to happen in two weeks, do not run and blabber to your team members about the layoff. First, understand the details of the layoff. Does it affect your team members? This kind of information flow can be very demoralizing to a team. Then announce the upcoming layoff with details in a team meeting at an appropriate time.

LESSONS LEARNED FROM THIS PROJECT EVENT

- Do not get your customers and your subcontractors involved in every little detail of your project.
- Filter your information appropriately in order to not inadvertently rock your project's boat.
- Learn the details of a demoralizing fact before discussing it with your project team members.

Case 1.16: Holiday Conflict with a Technical Proposal Presentation

We prepared a very competitive proposal for a large corporation in India. The proposal was for a pipeline communication system design, build, and installation. One of the bidding requirements was to make a technical presentation to the Indian company's bid evaluation committee in India. We sent our engineering vice president and a senior engineer to India to give our technical presentation. The Indian company confirmed the technical presentation time, duration, date, and location by e-mail three weeks before our team left the United States. Our technical presentation team arrived in Mumbai a day earlier. The next day, they went to the headquarters of the Indian company where the presentation was supposed to take place. There were only security guards at the entrance to the company compound. The guards told our team that the company was on holiday for three days for the Diwali festival and that there was no one from the bid evaluation committee working at the company that day.

Our team had no choice but to wait for three days until the holiday was over. Our presentation team called us and explained the miscommunication regarding the technical presentation date. We agreed with their decision to stay in Mumbai and reschedule the technical presentation with the Indian company. They toured Mumbai during the holidays and enjoyed the Diwali festival of lights and festivities. After three days, they called the chairman of the bid evaluation committee. He was very apologetic about the miscommunication regarding the technical presentation date. He said that he would like to talk to all bid evaluation committee members and set a new time and date as early as possible. He asked our team to call them back the next day.

The next day our team called the bid evaluation committee chairman. He set up the meeting the following day at 2 p.m. and also confirmed the new meeting time and date by e-mail. Our team was able to give their technical presentation five days after their arrival in Mumbai. Our team's presentation was scheduled for an hour. Afterward, an hour was reserved for a question and answer period. After the technical presentation meeting we received feedback from our team that all went well. However, we lost the bid to a French company with a lower cost basis. Our company spent over $100,000 to prepare for the bid and perform the required technical presentation. It was my mistake that I did not reconfirm the technical presentation time and date before our team left the United States. In international meeting setups, reconfirmation is a must. Things change fast and mistakes are made. A meeting set up a couple of weeks or months before might not be valid anymore. Continual communication among the involved parties and reconfirmation of the times and dates of meetings avoids mistakes and unnecessary headaches.

This is especially true in countries like India, as most religious holidays are according to the lunar calendar. Their dates change every year according to our Gregorian calendar. India has both national holidays and religious holidays. The national holidays such as Republic Day, Independence Day, and Mahatma Gandhi's birthday are fixed according to the Gregorian calendar. However, the religious holidays such as Hindu holidays, Parsee holidays, Islamic holidays, Sikh holidays, Buddhist holidays, and Jain holidays might shift dates every year in the Gregorian calendar. Also, depending upon the belief of the person(s) you are going to visit in India, some might be on his or her religious holiday, but the rest of the organization might be at work. In some countries, if a religious holiday comes on a Tuesday, Wednesday, and Thursday, the company you are dealing with or the entire country might decide to take the whole week off. They shut down their operations during Monday and Friday too, due to inefficiencies in the workplace and close down for a week. The whole country shuts down for a week.

For a global project manager, keeping track of all national and religious holidays of countries that you are dealing with is a requirement. You also have to know the religious beliefs of every individual you are dealing with. If you slack on keeping track of all national and religious holidays, an engineer you are dealing with in India might believe in Judaism and take a couple of days off during Hanukkah, the festival of lights, which might coincide with your scheduled visiting days to India.

LESSONS LEARNED FROM THIS PROJECT EVENT

- In a global project, know all the national and religious holidays of countries you are dealing with and record them in your project schedule.
- In a global project, know all religious observances of the people you are dealing with.

Case 1.17: Customer's Final Inspection Report

We completed on time the designing, manufacturing, and testing of mooring equipment and spare parts for a new oil rig on Sakhalin Island, Russia. The oil rig was being constructed in South Korea. Our equipment and spare parts were scheduled to ship to South Korea for installation onto the platform that was being built there. The customer's inspectors came to our facilities for final acceptance of all equipment and spare parts. The acceptance process took five days. With some minor modifications, everything was accepted and was ready to be shipped. We packaged all of the equipment and spare parts in waterproof crates and shipped them using a land/ocean route to South Korea. We included the inspector's final inspection report with the shipment. The final inspection report included the packing list of all the equipment and spare parts. We had a very experienced freight forwarder who insured the goods that were being shipped against all risks of physical loss or damage for door-to-door transportation. My customer's project manager was very satisfied with our performance. He released our milestone payment. My company got a hefty contract milestone payment of 50% of the contract value.

Five weeks passed and I received a call from my customer's project manager that the shipment had arrived in Pusan, South Korea, but they could not clear the cargo through South Korean customs because the spare parts were missing from the final inspection report's packing list. I told my customer's project manager that I would investigate the issue and get back to him in an hour. I went to our shipping department and found the packing list that our shipping department prepared for that shipment. Lo and behold, 10 spare part items were missing from the packing list. My shipping department missed the spare parts from the packing list. The customer's inspectors missed inspecting the spare parts. The bank that paid us our milestone payment missed the spare parts in the packing list. Now all of the equipment, close to 100 items, and 10 spare parts were sitting at South Korean customs and could not be cleared.

I called my customer's project manager and relayed the unfortunate chain of events. We brainstormed the situation at hand over the phone and tried to find a solution to the problem. One option was to ship the 10 spare parts that were not on the packing list back to the United States, get them inspected, and reship them back to South Korea with a correct packing list. This option would take about two months and would incur an extra cost of about $20,000. With this option, all of the equipment components could be cleared through customs in a timely fashion, but not the spare parts. The second option was to send a revised packing list to my customer's representative in South Korea. He could then present the revised packing list to South Korean customs and clear everything through customs. The only drawback with this option was that the 10 spare parts were not going to see the required final inspection per the project contract. I assured him that all those 10 spare parts were tested and inspected by our quality assurance department before final inspection took place. I left the decision to my customer's project manager. I told him that

I would go either way he chose to solve the issue at hand. He told me that he would discuss the two options with his superiors and get back to me the next day with a decision.

The next day, my customer's project manager called and told me that they had decided to go with option two. They could not live with a two-month delay in receiving the inspected spare parts. I was to revise the packing list in a day and send him a copy, and to his representative in South Korea the original by FedEx. He released us from the final inspection of spare parts by confirming their decision in an e-mail.

As the project manager I should have checked all final documents that went with the shipment. After this mishap, I made it a task for myself to review all documents that were included in a shipment for a customer. This was an honest mistake. My shipping department, the customer's inspectors, and my customer's bank, all missed the 10 spare parts from the packing list. Spare parts were in the list of deliverables, loud and clear, in our project's contract.

LESSONS LEARNED FROM THIS PROJECT EVENT

- The customer's final inspection report has to be scrutinized by you for accuracy.
- Simple errors in a customer's final inspection report can come back to bite you later in your project.

Case 1.18: Pressure Put on a Team Member by Upper Management

One of the mechanical design engineers on my project team was working on a wheelchair access ramp design for a bus. His design, manufacture, and test tasks were on the critical path of the project. I met with him weekly to see if he had any showstopping issues. I asked my other team members to help him in certain auxiliary tasks such as sourcing double-acting air actuated cylinders. He was determined to finish his design on time and he was putting in extra hours in order not to fall behind schedule.

One of our vice presidents from the sales department was going to his cubicle almost daily and asking him questions about his design and trying to get a feeling for the status of the wheelchair access ramp design. This vice president won the bus contract for our company. He felt as if the contract was his baby. He wanted everything to be completed on time so that he could satisfy our customer. He wanted to get more future contracts from our customer. The vice president was spending about half an hour with him at each visit. I was starting to get annoyed with his visits; but more than me, my design engineer was getting annoyed too. My design engineer was a nice guy and he did not complain to me for about a month. During one of our weekly status meeting, he finally spilled the beans and told me that he was sick and tired of the vice president's visits day in and day out. The vice president's visits to his cubicle were not constructive at all. He was wasting my design engineer's valuable time. He asked me to straighten out the situation.

I went to my boss and explained the unfortunate events between the sales vice president and my design engineer. We discussed how we should approach the vice president and ask him to end his daily meetings with my design engineer. We decided that I should go alone and talk to the vice president and explain to him the criticality of my design engineer's tasks. I was to ask him politely without offending him to end his daily visits to my design engineer's cubicle. I was to also offer to the vice president that he was more than welcome to visit my office daily to get an update regarding the status of the wheelchair access ramp design.

I made an appointment with him to discuss the criticality of the wheelchair access ramp design on the overall project. The meeting went well. He agreed that my design engineer's time was very valuable. We did not want my design engineer's critical tasks to fall behind and to cause a delay in the overall project. He was very receptive to my suggestion of getting daily status updates from me instead of visiting my design engineer's cubicle.

I relayed the results of our meeting to my boss and to my design engineer. My design engineer was relieved. As the project progressed he needed constant support in order to stay on schedule. He completed all the wheelchair access ramp design specifications, calculations, and drawings successfully two weeks late. I invited the sales vice president to the design review meeting. He did not have any comments or suggestions during the meeting, but he was nice enough to congratulate my design engineer for his thorough job. I also thanked the sales vice president for his overwhelming interest in our project and by coming daily to my office for the project updates. My project team caught up with the project schedule by working overtime during the manufacturing phase of the project.

In every project, almost all hands in a company swarm around a critical project person with good intentions to get a feeling for how things are going. They waste his or her valuable time. If the project person has an easygoing personality, he or she tries to accommodate everyone's inquiries and questions. Valuable time can be wasted and the project schedule can unintentionally go down the drain. You have to caution your team members to let you know if there are unnecessary interferences with their work. As a project manager, you have to protect your team members from these unnecessary distractions.

LESSONS LEARNED FROM THIS PROJECT EVENT

- As project managers, we have to protect our team members from pressure coming from outside our team environment.
- Time wasted by your team members due to outside interference can easily delay your project.

Case 1.19: Dictatorial Micromanagement

We had six program managers in the chip design section of my company. My company hired a new director of program managers from a well-established Silicon Valley company. He was a well-known authority in data chip design. He had started his job two months ago and started to enforce his style of management. I reported directly to him.

My boss had a dictatorial character. Everything was supposed to be done the way he saw it. He never listened to me or to my team members. He attended some of my weekly team meetings. He took over the whole show. My team members and I tried to give our input to solve an issue. He listened to our input half-heartedly. He countered with his own ideas and he demanded that our approach to a solution should be his way. I discussed his behavior with the other five program managers. He behaved the same with his dictatorial style of management to all of them.

Sometimes he went behind my back and talked to my engineers. He changed their ways of approaching an issue without informing me. I told him several times not to circumvent me and not to give mixed signals to my team members. He said "okay okay" to me and kept enforcing his own style of management.

My boss's behavior was demoralizing to my team. They started to hold themselves back and they started to not give any input whenever he joined our meetings. This was totally opposite of my management style. I promoted empowerment of my team members and everyone else contributing to my project. I listened to all input and chose the most logical approach. I treated my people with respect and consideration. I told my team members to hang in there and asked them to provide their suggestions and input regarding our project to me. I told them that I would deal with the director myself in protecting my team's suggestions and input. I used to have a weekly one-on-one meeting with the director. I defended my team members' suggestions and input. He started shouting and swearing and insisted that everything was to be done his way.

I could not take his one-man-show behavior anymore. I made an appointment with the vice president of human resources and detailed my concerns to her. I told her that our people were the most valuable asset of our company. I told her that my team members, other program managers, and I were fed up with the dictatorial behavior of our director. I emphasized that we could lose some of our crucial assets, if the director's behavior did not improve. She told me that she was aware of the situation. She had received other complaints about the director's authoritarian management style too. She asked me to sit tight and to keep the director away from my team members as much as I could. She promised me that there were going to be several big personnel changes coming very soon.

The following week there was a layoff at my company. My company dismissed 10% of the workforce including the director of program managers due to a slowdown in business. The dictator was gone in three months. Everyone in the company was very happy. My team members began to get motivated again. I respected and encouraged their input. I continually tried to develop my team members' brainstorming and engineering skills so that I could extract the highest possible performance from each one of them. I always wanted to create a culture and environment that supported and respected my people.

The company promoted a director of program managers from within the company. The new director's management style was very much like mine. We got along great. My team members performed flawlessly to complete my project on time and within budget. I was lucky that three months of a distasteful ordeal with the authoritarian director did not hamper my project.

During my 40-year engineering and management career, I came across many different styles of managing people. The worst management style belonged to this director who was micromanaging everyone under him in an authoritarian fashion.

LESSONS LEARNED FROM THIS PROJECT EVENT

- A dictatorial boss can overwhelm you and your project team and cause damage to your project without realizing the consequences.
- You have to protect your project team from your authoritarian boss at all costs.
- You have to take immediate steps to correct your boss's unacceptable behavior.

Case 1.20: Setting Up Two Automated Assembly Modules in Malaysia

Labor costs were increasing fast in our Malaysian plant. Also, computer component sizes were shrinking and their assembly and alignment tolerances were getting tighter and tighter to the order of ± 0.0001 inches or ± 2.5 micrometers. I was assigned to develop an automated assembly module for our computer component assembly processes and get two modules into operation in Malaysia. I was assigned two full-time senior manufacturing engineers from our U.S. plant to my team. Our first task was to search in the United States for an automation development house and get the automated assembly module built to our specifications. After a three-month search, we found an automation subcontractor in Boston whose cost proposal and whose technical capabilities fit our mission.

I made a half-hour presentation to my company's board of directors about our options and their return on investment and got the automation project approved. Our board's approval was a requirement for projects over $2M dollars. This was the highest-priced project for the company and it had to be completely installed and in operation in Malaysia in nine months. All the automation drawings had to be in both British and in metric units. All fasteners had to be in metric so that they could be easily sourced in Malaysia. I sent two of my engineers to Boston and made them live with the project at the subcontractor's plant day in and day out. I also had to find three Malaysian engineers who were mechanically savvy so that I could bring them for the automation module qualification runs to Boston for three months. They were going to be trained in-depth for the operation and maintenance of the automated assembly modules by the subcontractor. These three Malaysian engineers would ultimately be responsible for running the automated assembly modules in our Malaysian plant.

I communicated with our Malaysian general manager and sent him the requirements for the Malaysian engineers. They found nine candidates. I traveled to Malaysia to interview the nine candidates face to face. The Malaysian general manager and I agreed, after interviewing all the nine candidates, to hire three of the candidates. These Malaysian engineers were also responsible for writing the equipment operation and maintenance manuals in English and in Bahasa Malay. I made sure that they had the correct entry visas into the United States for three months. I arranged for an apartment for them within walking distance to our subcontractor's plant. They traveled to Boston after six months into the project when the module was getting ready for the qualification runs. During those six months in Malaysia, they prepared the site for two automated assembly modules. The site had to have temperature and humidity control and had to have a class 100 clean room environment. The site floor had to be vibration-free and the power supply had to have voltage regulators and the power supply had to be uninterruptible. They also had to source a precision machine shop close to our plant in Malaysia for precision spare tools.

Everything was on schedule and within my cost prediction for the first six months of the project. When we started to assemble and test the system we started to have clogging problems with the automated epoxy dispensing unit. In our specifications, we required a periodic maintenance for half an hour at every eight hours to the automated assembly modules, namely at the beginning of every shift. However, the epoxy temperature control and dispensing required the system to be cleaned and maintained every hour. This was totally unacceptable because it reduced our throughput from the assembly system by 25%. It took our subcontractor and the project team another three months to find an acceptable solution to the epoxy dispensing unit's short operating cycle. With better temperature control and with a modified epoxy dispensing unit, the periodic maintenance interval was increased from one hour to four hours. During this unfortunate event, the cost of the project soared by 40% and I had to go in front of the board again to explain the failing adhesive dispensing submodule and the proposed solutions and to ask for a three-month extension and a 40% cost increase for my project. That was a painful experience to face the board members, but the company board realized that there was a light at the end of the tunnel and shelving the project at this juncture would have been more harmful for our company.

After a three-month delay, the qualification runs in Boston started and went well. The Malaysian engineers learned the system hands on and in great detail. However, we had to accept the automated assembly modules with a four-hour periodic maintenance interval that resulted in a 6% throughput loss. I had to again go in front of the company board to explain the final status of the automated assembly modules. I got their approval to accept the system with 6% throughput loss, not to push our subcontractor to meet the system specifications to the letter, and not to delay the project further out.

We shipped two unassembled automated assembly modules by air to Malaysia to gain time. We reassembled the two systems in Malaysia and started to make qualification runs. Two engineers from our subcontractor, two engineers from my team, three Malaysian engineers, and myself got two automated assembly modules ready for production in two weeks in Malaysia.

There were some other unforeseen glitches in the Malaysian operation of the two automation assembly modules. One glitch was with the spare parts. In a three-shift operation a day and six days a week, we were always short of spare parts. We had to increase our spare parts supply by twofold in a hurry. Also, we had to set up a two-day delivery system with Federal Express from the United States from several of our automated assembly module's component manufacturers.

Another issue in Malaysia was with one of the Malaysian engineers. He had to leave the company for medical reasons. I had to scramble and get one of the U.S.-based engineers on my team to go to Malaysia and support them in the operation and maintenance of the systems. He had to live in Malaysia for six months until another Malaysian engineer was found and properly trained. The Malaysian plant's general manager was very helpful in finding a new Malaysian engineer.

Another nagging issue was the shortage of computer components for assembly for a given customer. Some of the components were delayed in customs or at the original manufacturer. Some of the component lots were rejected at the receiving inspection stage. Initially, two automated assembly modules were idle about 15% of the time in a given month. The Malaysian plant had to increase the inventory of the computer components that had to be assembled for a specific customer. After six months of operation and a diligent component inventory control, the two automated assembly modules' idle time was reduced to 4%.

After operating the two automated assembly modules for one month in production, the precision alignment pins started to wear out. Computer component assembly locations started to shift. I requested our subcontractor to come to Malaysia urgently. We put our heads together and decided that we had to replace all of the precision alignment pins with ones that were made out of harder material. We updated all the affected drawings and were able to source the new harder precision pins in Germany. This retrofit to the two systems took two weeks and it made the automated assembly modules' operation much more stable.

After we qualified the two automation assembly modules, we had to invite our customers to our plant in Malaysia for production qualification runs for their specific computer component assemblies. One of our customers was Japanese and the other was French. We first brought the Japanese customer's representatives into our plant and showed them our new automation assembly module. We made a shift's worth of assembly runs for them, about 1,000 assemblies. We measured the critical parameters of all the assemblies and studied their means and spreads. The means were very close to the customer's specification nominal. The spreads were about 50% narrower than the manual assembly control charts. The Japanese customer accepted the new automation assembly module without any reservations. The following week, we performed a similar qualification process for our French customer. The French customer's qualification also went smoothly.

After 14 months of challenging problem-solving sessions, board meetings, communications, and travel between our U.S. plant in California, our subcontractor in Boston, and our plant in Malaysia, my project team, our subcontractor, and the Malaysian project team did a great job of developing and implementing the two automation assembly modules in our Malaysian plant.

LESSONS LEARNED FROM THIS PROJECT EVENT

- The difficulties in setting up automated assembly lines in developing countries.
- As a project manager, details of a task are very crucial. An issue can always pop up that you might have easily overlooked.
- Budget overruns are a part of life for a project manager. How to deal with them in a timely fashion is a must.

- It is sometimes not feasible to comply with every specification of your project. You have to go to your customer and ask for deviations using justifiable reasoning.
- You have to learn the infrastructure and capabilities of each one of your team's personnel in utmost detail in all foreign countries that you are dealing with.

Case 1.21: Project Closure—Lessons Learned Meetings

I was in the process of closing out a two-year project in advanced electric bus design and manufacturing. My final project status report was accepted by my customer. I presented the final project metrics to the domestic and international upper management of my company. I received a favorable final project evaluation report from my customer's project manager. Everything regarding the project's closure was going smoothly. Then, I was called to an emergency fire-fighting mission to South Korea. I had to travel to South Korea immediately and ended up staying there for three weeks in order to straighten out my company's urgent issue with a casting subcontractor. The only thing that was left open from my project's closure was the lessons learned meetings with my team members, with my domestic and international upper management, with my customer's project manager, and with my subcontractors.

When I returned to the United States, I compiled a list of lessons learned items from my two-year project. I tried to get a meeting going with my old team members, but everyone was assigned to other project teams and it was difficult to come up with a common meeting time. Also, interest in such project closure meetings faded away fast. Everyone involved had different pressing priorities. Two of my team members were assigned to a project in Japan. Finally, I was able to gather eight out of ten team members to a luncheon meeting. Of course, I promised to buy lunch for everyone. I presented my lessons learned list. We discussed what to do in the future in order not to fall into similar situations. I later did the same presentation to two engineers residing in Japan via videoconferencing. I gave a similar lessons learned presentation to my team members in Germany via videoconferencing. Then I called a lessons learned meeting for my upper management team to which only half of the upper managers attended. I also called my customer's project manager and my major subcontractors to discuss pertinent portions of my lessons learned list. Finally, I released the lessons learned list with constructive input from all my contacts into document control so that all future project managers could easily access it. It took me a good part of a week to complete my final duties for my completed project. I charged my time to the company overhead account because all project numbers were already closed.

The final lessons learned list covered issues related to team personnel, project specifications, my company, my customer, my subcontractors, project schedule, and project budget. In all of the issues discussed during our lessons learned meetings, two of them stood out and they were related to the project's cost. One lessons learned item was the price of the bus frames which were built by our subcontractor in Germany. We had to pay an extra 20% in U.S. dollars for those frames due to devaluation of the U.S. dollar against the Euro. In an international project like that one, my company should have analyzed the future value of the U.S. dollar against the Euro and should have bought Euros at the beginning of the project to cover the cost of all bus frames. In our future global projects, our chief financial officer was very careful in dealing with my company's liabilities in different foreign currencies. After this lessons learned event, my company bought sufficient futures in different foreign currencies against the U.S. dollar that were required for our global projects.

The second lessons learned cost issue was due to the price increase in special high-strength steel purchases. During the course of the project, the price of special high-strength steel increased substantially due to increasing worldwide demand. Our purchasing department bought the steel in three segments from three different customer-approved sources due to our tight cash flow. This strategy worked against us as the price of steel skyrocketed. We should have bought all of the required steel at the beginning of the project or we should have bargained with one steel supplier to deliver the required amount in three installments at the same initial price. Again, our purchasing strategies were improved and scrutinized very carefully after this lessons learned event.

Closing a project appropriately can be painful and time consuming. However, rewards of a properly closed project can be invaluable. Lessons learned from a completed project can be one of the most important items on a project closure to-do list. As project managers, we have to finalize lessons learned meetings at all costs even if the interest in the completed project is quickly fading away.

LESSONS LEARNED FROM THIS PROJECT EVENT

- Lessons learned from the execution of a project should be documented and presented to everyone who played a part in your project.
- After a project winds down, it is difficult to get your old team together for a meeting.

Case 1.22: Penalties in a Project Contract

Penalties in a project contract can come with quite different wording and meaning. As global project managers we have to fully understand the meaning of these penalties. We need to bring our lawyers into the picture if we have to clarify or modify certain contract clauses. Then we have to relay all of the information related to a project contract's penalties in detail to our team members and to our upper management. Liquidated damages are good examples of a project contract's penalties.

In one of my project contracts, the liquidated damages were worded as follows:

> If Seller does not deliver goods in conditions stipulated and in accordance with delivery times provided in this Contract, Purchaser is entitled to recover reasonable liquidated damages per each week of delay.

This was a vague penalty statement. What was the meaning of *reasonable*? Who decided on the "reasonable" damage? I had to get this statement modified before the start of the project. I got my upper management and my legal department involved to clear up this vagueness in the contract. After two weeks of negotiations with the customer, the final version of the contract for liquidated damages read as follows:

> If Seller does not deliver goods in conditions stipulated in this contract and in accordance with delivery times provided in this Contract, Purchaser will recover 4% of the total purchase price per each week of delay as liquidated damages. A delivery delay in goods caused by a force majeure impediment is excluded from liquidated damages.

In another project contract, a penalty clause was stipulated as follows:

> Seller is obliged to deliver all goods according to packing, preservation and marking instructions of Purchaser. If Seller does not carry out these instructions, Purchaser is entitled to a price reduction of 5% of the total contract price.

I reviewed the entire contract in order to find these instructions, but there were none. I called my customer's project manager and discussed missing packing, preservation, and marking instructions. We agreed on all the details in such a way that the price of the contract did not change. He sent me a written confirmation of all packing, preservation, and marking instructions. I was relieved to finalize a missing item from my project's contract before it was too late.

In a chip design project contract, the following contract statement was very restrictive to the progress of my project in a timely fashion.

> Purchaser shall have the right to request changes from this contract agreement. Seller shall not proceed with any such change until an official change order is received from the Purchaser.

This clause was impossible to implement. The chip design specifications were very fluid. My team members and my customer's engineers conferred daily for specification clarifications and for additions and deletions to specifications. The project could not progress if I waited for an official change order from my customer for every specification change event. I discussed this showstopper clause with my customer's project manager. We agreed to modify this contract clause as follows:

> Purchaser shall have the right to request changes from this contract agreement. Seller shall not proceed with any such change until an e-mail describing the change is received from the Purchaser's Project Manager. All changes approved by e-mails shall be collected monthly into an official change order by the Purchaser.

In one of my offshore oil platform equipment delivery projects, the contract stipulated the delivery time as the date the equipment in question was installed and was operational on the platform. If I missed that date I was penalized by a liquidated damage clause in my contract. I had to watch like a hawk for any equipment installation delays caused by my customer. Several times their power lines were not ready. On one occasion they had to perform extensive welding, which blockaded the area of our equipment installation. I recorded all these delays caused by my customer and immediately informed my customer's project manager so that I would not get penalized for events that were beyond my control.

Penalties in a project's contract can be ambiguous, too general, vague, inconsistent, redundant, and conflicting. As global project managers, we have to catch these sinkholes before the execution of our contracts and have them clarified without any reservations.

LESSONS LEARNED FROM THIS PROJECT EVENT

- As project managers, we have to fully understand all penalties written into our project's contract.
- We have to get vaguely worded contract penalties well defined by our customer and if necessary with the help of our legal department.
- We have to explain project penalties and their consequences to our team members, to our upper management, and to our subcontractors at the beginning of our projects.

2

CASE STUDIES IN SCOPE MANAGEMENT

As project managers, we have to watch the scope of a project like a hawk and we have to be the final authority for the project's scope changes. Changes and misinterpretations of a project's scope can occur very easily behind our backs.

In a chip design project, the specifications were written in a very concise fashion and they were open to many interpretations. As the design progressed, my team started to have numerous questions about the specifications that needed clarification. Also, my customer in Germany wanted to add several enhancements to the chip design along the way. Specifications that are in a constant flux can be very challenging to control as depicted in Case 2.1.

During the manufacturing phase of a research safety vehicle project, there was a sudden program manager change with our customer. The new program manager was clueless about the history of the program. He started to demand changes to the vehicle design that were above and beyond the specification clarifications and changes we had agreed to with his predecessor. As project manager, I had to put the brakes on and bring him back to reality in my project as detailed in Case 2.2.

In a fixed price contract, the customer's specifications had quite a few TBDs (to be determined items). For a project manager, TBDs required a lot of attention and caused tremendous headaches between the customer's project manager and myself. I had to watch these TBDs like a hawk. When a TBD specification was finalized by the customer, I had to make sure that the clarified specification was doable and that it did not affect my project's cost and time constraints as shown in Case 2.3.

In one project, I had dual customers and therefore two customers' project managers. To keep both customers' project managers in sync and happy took a lot of extra effort during the execution of my project.

I detail the issues I encountered with the dual customers' project managers in Case 2.4.

We had to finish the manufacturing phase of a project destined for Russia by the end of January so that we could test and ship the heavy equipment mover system for installation and training during the summer months there. Our customer's project manager called me and told me that several of their other subcontractors were delayed in completing their tasks. They also had some cash flow issues so they wanted to delay our mover system to be installed during the following summer's window. A year delay to complete a project requires several adjustments to tasks as shown in Case 2.5.

I took over a project right in the middle of its design phase. My customer's project manager was accustomed to calling my team's design engineers and ordering minor variations to the specifications on the telephone without my knowledge. Nothing was documented and we were drifting away from the original project technical specifications. Apparently, the previous project manager closed his eyes to these minor specification variations and my customer's project manager became used to forcing these minor specification changes on my design engineers as detailed in Case 2.6.

I had several projects where minor scope changes occurred. I went along with my customer's requests without going through the mind-boggling change approval cycle. My customer's project manager followed a similar process. This was a documented bartering process of minor scope changes between my customer and me as detailed in Case 2.7.

Software used in a project has to be scrutinized for compatibility very carefully. There can be many unforeseen conflicts and issues between customers, subcontractors, and internal users of software. I ran into several serious issues with software as detailed in Case 2.8.

Case 2.1: Specification Clarifications with a Customer in Germany

I had a nine-month project to develop the software for a mobile phone wireless application connectivity chipset for a German customer. I had six chip software design and test engineers working on my team on a full-time basis. Our offices were in California and my customer's offices were in Munich, Germany. This nine-hour difference in the time zones brought to the surface several communication challenges, especially as the chipset specifications were written in a very concise fashion and they were open to many interpretations. As the design progressed, my team started to have numerous questions about the specifications that needed clarifications. Also, the customer wanted to add on several enhancements to the chipset design along the way.

I was lucky that this custom chipset software development project was not a fixed price contract. It was a time and materials agreement. I had to inform the customer weekly of how his money was being spent on the project. There were no punishing scope changes and specification revisions. I only had to record every specification clarification and every additional specification enhancement as the project moved on. This custom software development project required precision and on-time communication methods with the customer. These communication methods had to eliminate any specification ambiguities in their fluid state.

At the project kickoff meeting with the customer, I offered to have a daily one-hour telecommunication with my team and on his end with him and the others that he wanted to bring into the teleconference from Monday through Friday. The teleconference time would be at 8 a.m. Pacific standard time, which would make it 5 p.m. in Munich, Germany. He accepted my meeting proposal. I also proposed that we both record the teleconference proceedings so that we would not miss any specification clarifications, additions, or deletions. I also told the customer's project manager that I would review the meeting tape recordings daily and summarize the contents and issue the meeting minutes by e-mail to him for his approval within 24 hours. I would update the chipset design specifications weekly, release the new revision to our document control, and distribute them to the customer's project manager and to my team. The customer's project manager was very happy with my specification control procedures. We started the project this way.

After the second week into the project, I started seeing delays in my engineers' performance. Specification clarifications and customer's additions or deletions were not being handled on a timely basis. This was such a dynamic project that my engineers required instant clarifications and solutions to specifications. My team and customer's interface had to be in more real time. We could not wait 24 hours to get a response from the customer for specification clarifications. The communication setup was bogging down my engineers and hampering their progress.

I had a team meeting to discuss the specifications and customer interface issues. Two of my senior software engineers offered to change their schedule and work a swing shift from 6 p.m. to 3 a.m. from Sunday night through Thursday night. They were used to these kinds of odd work hours from university days. They thought they would be more productive by not being disturbed by other colleagues in the office. This setup would give my team four hours of direct interface with Germany from 11 p.m. to 3 a.m. These two software designers were responsible for the most critical segments of the chipset. I told them that their proposal would be a great solution for our team's progress. This new setup would give us five hours of real-time interface with the customer. My condition was that they had to tape record every conversation with the customer so that I could collect all the clarifications and changes regarding the chipset specifications. Also, I would have a meeting with these two engineers from 6 p.m. to 7 p.m., Sunday through Thursday, in order to review their progress, to discuss the issues they were having, to give them updates as to what was happening during the day shift, and to bring them up to date from the results of my morning call with our customer.

I told them we would propose our new interface setup to our customer's project manager in the morning. I also told them that I would discuss new working hours with their supervisors and with human resources so that there were no hidden kinks in the new proposal. There could have been company security issues. There could have been overtime payment requirements. These engineers were salaried engineers and there was no overtime work adjustment to their salaries. The supervisors of the two engineers and human resources found no drawbacks for them to work from 6 p.m. to 3 a.m., Sunday through Thursday night, for the duration of my project.

The next morning, during our teleconference with our customer, we discussed the new working hours of my two senior engineers and how this new setup would improve real-time communication to clarify ambiguities in specifications. The customer's project manager was very receptive to our proposal. My two engineers started to work in the swing shift and this new setup increased our real-time communication with the customer to five hours a day. This new setup was very effective in getting quick responses to questions regarding chipset design specifications and it lasted for six months. Also, these two software designers worked very efficiently without being disturbed.

My team finished the chipset software design and test on time. I generated a complete set of specifications for the chipset which was up to date. My customer appreciated the complete set of specifications tremendously. At the end of the project, I wrote a resounding recommendation for the two software engineers who had volunteered to work the swing shift. The beauty of this solution was that the swing shift idea came from the engineers. This was a win-win situation for my project, for my company, and above all for the customer.

LESSONS LEARNED FROM THIS PROJECT EVENT

- In a global project environment, real-time communication between your team and your customer might require unusual work schedules.
- As project managers, we have to notify our project team members' supervisors and get their approval for changing work schedules.
- Keeping track of all changing project specifications and their clarifications during the execution of a global project can be very time consuming.

Case 2.2: A Change in the Customer's Program Manager in the Middle of a Project

I was the project manager for the research safety vehicle development for the National Highway Traffic Safety Administration, an agency for the Department of Transportation. The design phase of the project was completed. We started to manufacture prototype vehicles and got them ready for crash testing. During the course of the design and development process, there were many specification clarifications and changes to the vehicle. All specification clarifications and changes were document controlled in our company. Every revised version of the specifications was submitted to our customer.

During the manufacturing phase of the project, there was a sudden program manager change with our customer. The new program manager was clueless about the history of the research safety vehicle program. He started to demand changes to the vehicle design that were above and beyond the specification clarifications and changes we agreed upon with his predecessor. He wanted specification changes in the vehicle's ground clearance, the vehicle's maximum curb weight, the vehicle's side impact crashworthiness, and so on. The vehicle design had already been completed and it was not possible to implement his new specification requests at this stage of the project. When I refused to implement some of the changes that he requested, things started to get tense between us. I sensed a rising tension from his tone during our telephone conferences. I had to do something urgently to bring this customer's new program manager to our level of understanding of vehicle specifications and contract requirements.

I decided that I could not bring him up to date from 3,000 miles away in our research safety vehicle project, which had been going on for three years. I kindly asked him to plan a trip to come to our facilities in California and spend a week with us so that he could meet my team members and could see our operations and capabilities in person. My main purpose was to go over the history of the project step by step with him. I wanted him to understand all the specification clarifications and changes that were made during those three years. The customer's new program manager accepted my proposal, decided to leave his desk behind in Washington, DC, and visit our facilities.

I sent him a proposed agenda for his visit. He accepted all of my proposed agenda with some minor variations. The first day was dedicated to meeting my team members and our upper management. On the second day, we concentrated on our manufacturing facilities and our test facilities. On the third and fourth days, we went through the history of the research safety vehicle project. We went over every specification one by one. We reviewed all the specification clarifications. We reviewed all the new specifications that were added on by my team or by his predecessor. Then we reviewed every contract modification and every monthly status report. He was very impressed with our precise document control procedures.

On the fifth day, we went over the master project schedule and reviewed tasks that were on the critical path. He was brought up to speed on every aspect of the project. He was very appreciative of such a detailed project review. I was ecstatic too that he was finally at the same level of understanding of the project as me and my team.

By the afternoon of the fifth day, we had covered everything we could regarding the project and we deserved a break from work. I took him to our city center for lunch and I played tour guide and showed him the highlights of our city. During this interaction, I learned a lot about the personal side of my customer's new program manager. He was also a tennis buff like me. Later, I invited him to play an hour of tennis with me. I provided him with all the tennis gear. The customer's new program manager left California with a good understanding of the research safety project. He gained trust in our project team and in our project processes. Above all, he became a project contributing colleague and a good friend.

These kinds of changes to critical personnel can happen in any project. It is the project manager's responsibility to bring the new team member up to speed about the project.

LESSONS LEARNED FROM THIS PROJECT EVENT

- Bringing your customer's new project manager up to speed might need patience and require careful planning and execution.
- Mutual trust and respect established between you and your customer's project manager along with a personal touch are signs of a matured project manager.

Case 2.3: TBD and Erroneous Specifications for a Project

We were doing a mooring system project for an offshore oil rig in the Gulf of Mexico. It was a fixed price contract, but the specifications were sprinkled with a lot of TBDs (to be determined) items. As the project manager, the TBDs required a lot of attention and caused tremendous headaches between the customer's project manager and myself. I had to watch these TBDs like a hawk. When a TBD specification was finalized by the customer, I had to ensure that the clarified specification was doable and that it did not affect my project's cost and time constraints.

Out of a dozen TBD specifications, one was for the smoothness of a stainless steel surface. I had to negotiate this TBD specification rigorously with the customer's project manager. I did not want to accept a tight specification that would have required extra fine machining of stainless steel surfaces of our system. We first agreed on the smoothness measurement technique and then the measurement sampling location and measurement length for traces. Then we agreed on the maximum R_a value, maximum value of the arithmetic average of absolute values of vertical deviations of the roughness profile from the mean line. I sent my customer's project manager an e-mail outlining the agreed upon smoothness specification in detail and asked him to send me his approval note for this TBD specification. After I received his approval note, I initiated an engineering change order for the project specifications in our document control system. I distributed the final smoothness speci-fication to all the engineers and manufacturing people who were involved with the stainless steel surfaces. I also sent a copy of the released project specification to my customer's project manager.

One by one, we negotiated and agreed on all the TBD specifica-tions. One of these specifications was the interface drawings that were supposed to be delivered to us after four weeks from the start of the project. It took them six weeks to deliver the interface drawings to us. We were lucky to receive them in six weeks and fortunately, they did not affect the progress of my project. So I did not raise any ruckus with my customer about this crucial delay. I kept their delay as an ace in my pocket to exchange it with a future project delay that could have happened on our side.

We finished all our stress calculations and system components designs on time. We as a team were ready for the mooring sys-tem design review. We had a two-day meeting at our facilities. During the meeting, the customer's chief engineer told us that the slots that were designed into the mooring system were good for the chain passage, but they were not sized appropriately for the passage of the chain connectors. My team and I were quite sur-prised by this announcement by our customer, because the project specifications clearly identified the chain size and dimensions and also identified that there would be no chain connectors in this mooring system. I showed them their specifications. My custom-er's team was embarrassed to realize their slip in project specifi-cations. My customer's project manager emphasized that we had to redesign the mooring system for the chain connector passage.

The only solution was to evaluate the impact of this major change to our project for manpower, cost, and schedule. I asked my customer's project manager to give me two days to analyze the effects of this major change and to provide him with a written revised proposal. He accepted my offer and they left our facilities after throwing a major twist into the project. We had to redo all of our stress calculations and change our design drawings. On top of it all, I was not even sure if all the designers on my team were available for the expanding project.

I had a meeting with my team to get their time estimates for the customer's new change order. I estimated the time and cost impact of the engineering change order to the project. I met with the man-agers of each member of my team regarding their availability for the extended project. After I had all the facts, I collected my upper management team for a meeting and showed them the impact of our customer's change order. They made some minor changes to my cost estimates. I got the upper management's blessing for the change order. Then I wrote a formal response to my customer's project manager for their proposed change. The project was delayed by two months and this major slip in my customer's specifications cost them 20% extra.

My customer's project manager discussed my schedule and cost impact on the project to their change order with his upper management. They had no negotiation leverage but to accept my proposal. The surprising change order was a major slip on their part. My team finished the project two weeks earlier than promised. My team's efforts to finish the project two weeks early received excellent reviews from my customer's project manager.

LESSONS LEARNED FROM THIS PROJECT EVENT

- At the start of a project, there can be several TBD specifications in your customer's documents. As project managers, we have to have them clarified as soon as possible.
- Sometimes a customer's specifications can be in error or missing, which might change the course of your project.
- Any major project specification changes have to be analyzed very carefully and with the utmost detail by you and then presented to your upper management for their approval. Your presentation should cover change order effects on your team members, on the project schedule, and on the project cost. Then, the change order should be introduced to your customer.

Case 2.4: Dual Customer Project Managers for a Project

I was heading an electric bus design and manufacturing project for the municipal transit district of a large metropolitan city. It was a two-year project. My team had to design, build, and test 15 electric buses for operation in the city's downtown area as a free people mover. The 40-passenger buses had to have a range of 50 miles in a stop-and-go downtown environment before changing their batteries with a fully charged set. This was a dream and a leading-edge project in the 1980s. The project was sponsored by the Department of Transportation. The interesting part of the project was that I had two bosses for the project. One was the project manager from the Department of Transportation who sponsored the project and the other was the project manager from the city's municipal transit district who was going to utilize the electric buses.

We also had to deliver the buses to the city's municipal transit district and had to train their personnel for operation and maintenance of the buses. As a project manager, my duties were almost doubled. I had to communicate ins and outs of the project to both project managers. I had to keep both of them up to date regarding the project. Both project managers had to be present at all the critical meetings. Critical meetings had to be set up by considering both project managers' schedules. Whenever there was an engineering change order, both project managers had to sign it off. I had to keep track of all the correspondence with both project managers. These routine tasks were fine and dandy, but when the two project managers had conflicting ideas and demands about the project, things got out of hand. I acted as an ombudsman and tried to resolve the conflicting issues by having telephone conversations between the three of us. If telephone dialogue did not work out, I had to bring all three of us into a meeting room.

One of the conflicts came from the minimum ground clearance specification. The initial minimum ground clearance specification was 9 inches. All the design was done per this specification. During the design review meeting, the municipal transport district project manager requested this minimum ground clearance to be increased to 12 inches. I explained to them that at this stage of the project it would be difficult to change this specification and I explained the reasons. I told them if they insisted on increasing the minimum ground clearance of the buses, we had to redesign several subcomponents. This would delay the project by at least two months and it would also have a cost increase impact. The Department of Transportation project manager insisted that we stay with the original specification, but the municipal transport district project manager did not budge from his request. I saw that we were not going to resolve this conflict during the meeting. I requested a recess. I gathered the two project managers into a smaller conference room away from my project team. We discussed the pros and cons of increasing the minimum ground clearance specification in detail. I made the municipal transport district project manager agree to the fact that the city's downtown route was very flat with no dips or bumps. I also listed all the changes that had to be implemented in order to comply with his request. The Department of Transportation project manager allowed me to do all the talking and convincing. I asked both of them to sleep on this conflicting specification and to make a decision by tomorrow's design review meeting.

The next morning at the beginning of our design review meeting, both project managers announced that they agreed to stay with the original minimum ground clearance specification. This was quite a relief to me and to my project team.

Another conflict between the two project managers surfaced toward the end of the project about the driving cycles that were to be used to test buses for a range specification of 50 miles. We proposed to load a vehicle with fully charged batteries with sandbags to simulate 40 passengers and run it on an airport runway mimicking a city's downtown stop-and-go environment. The municipal transport district project manager bought into our proposal. He asked us to repeat the test three times with different buses in order to get an accurate understanding of the electric buses' range. This time, the Department of Transportation project manager had issues with my range test proposal. He wanted us to ship two completed buses to the city and run those two buses there for a week while transporting people, using its air conditioning, and operating its wheelchair ramps. He wanted a real life test in the city's downtown driving environment before accepting our buses. These proposed range tests were risky because of the uncontrolled environment. I had a teleconference with both project managers to discuss the range test process. After an hour of negotiating they both agreed that we would perform the controlled range tests as I proposed. Then after they accepted the buses, we would ship two buses to the city to be tested for range in the actual downtown environment. This agreement was a win-win agreement for both sides. We got what we wanted because my priority was the acceptance of the buses. The Department of Transportation project manager got what he wanted, too.

Both range tests were performed without a hitch. At the simulated range test, we got close to 60 miles of range. At the city's downtown range tests, we got higher ranges because the buses were not always fully loaded.

LESSONS LEARNED FROM THIS PROJECT EVENT

- As project managers, you can have more than one boss on your project's customer end.
- Conflicts can arise between your multiple bosses at the customer's end that can negatively affect the progress of your project.
- You might have to bring your multiple bosses together to discuss and to negotiate a just solution to the issue at hand.

Case 2.5: A Customer Delays Installation and Training

I was heading a two-year heavy equipment mover system project for Russia to be installed at a Siberian location. The project had four phases, which were design, manufacturing, testing and installation, and training. The design phase was completed in eight months on time and within budget. The critical design review was held in our facilities in the United States and it went very smoothly. We were in the nine-month manufacturing phase of the mover system. We had to finish the manufacturing phase by the end of January so that we could test and ship the mover system to Russia for installation and training during the summer months there. The customer gave us a four-month window for the installation and training phase in Siberia, namely, the months of May, June, July, and August.

We worked hard to complete manufacturing by the end of January. I had to authorize some overtime work due to several inefficiencies during the Christmas break. We were almost about to complete our manufacturing operations and the customer came to us with surprising news. Our customer's project manager called me and told me that several of their other subcontractors were delayed in completing their tasks. They also had some cash flow issues so they wanted to delay our mover system to be installed during the following summer's window. I told him that I would discuss this sudden shift of events with my upper management and would get back to him with my response in two days.

First, I collected my team for a meeting and discussed the implications of the installation and training delay for a year. Everyone on my team concurred that we should test the mover system in our facilities during February and March without delay and we should have our customer come to our facilities to accept the mover system. After the mover system was accepted we should crate the system for surface shipment. Then, we should find a storage space that was clean and that was temperature and humidity controlled to store the mover system for a year. We should also charge the mover system transfer and storage expenses to our customer.

Then I had a meeting with my upper management team to inform them of my customer's delay and to discuss my team's counterproposal to this delay. Upper management was very receptive to our proposal. A one-year delay in completing the project would have a minimal effect on our cash flow. All my team members would be allocated to other projects by the end of March.

Four of my engineers would be reassigned to my project the following May for installation and training in Siberia. We decided not to apply the penalty clause of the project agreement for their delaying the project. My upper management gave me the green light to make our counterproposal to our customer. During these internal negotiations with my upper management, I asked two of my engineers who had some slack time to investigate the expenses for a storage facility. We needed about 2,000 square feet of space for a year. They found a couple of alternative storage spots close to our facility. The mover system transfer and storage costs for a year were estimated to be between $40k and $50k.

The next day, I called our customer's project manager in London and gave him the details of our counterproposal. He also wanted to delay the acceptance tests, but I stood my ground in order not to delay the acceptance tests. I told him that we were not applying any penalty clauses of our agreement for their delay. And that we were doing extra work to find a storage space to store the mover system under very secure and favorable environmental conditions for a year for just $40k. He said he had to go back to his people and get their input for my counterproposal. I did not hear from him for two days. During this time, I put our counterproposal in an item-by-item written format and e-mailed it to him. I called him back to see what was going on. He asked for another week before he could make a decision on our counterproposal. During this time, we started testing the completed subsystems of the mover system. I allocated two months of testing and final acceptance for the completed mover system.

LESSONS LEARNED FROM THIS PROJECT EVENT

- Completion of your project can be delayed by your customer.
- Always get your project team involved for major changes and decisions to your project.
- Always get your upper management's approval for major changes and decisions to your project.
- Stand your ground with your customers during negotiations if the issue at hand is caused by them.

Case 2.6: Project Scope Changes

I was brought in as the project manager of an advanced vehicle development project during the detailed design phase. The previous project manager had to resign from our company due to health reasons. My customer was the U.S. Department of Transportation. I had a team of six automotive design engineers working on my team. When I came into the project, the first thing I did was to learn the advanced vehicle specifications and the deliverables' timeline. Then I learned the responsibilities and capabilities of every team member. I went to Washington, DC from California to meet with my customer's project manager and to generate a close rapport with him.

According to the original schedule, we were about two weeks late and the project was running over budget by 6% when I took over. One thing that bothered me was that my customer's project manager was accustomed to phoning my team's design engineers and ordering minor variations to the specifications without my knowledge. Nothing was documented and we were drifting away from the original project technical specifications. Apparently, the previous project manager closed his eyes to these minor specification variations and my customer's project manager got used to forcing these minor specification changes on my design engineers.

The first thing I did was to have an emergency team meeting. I went over all pending redlines that were not released through document control. The original specifications were still at revision A. I asked my team members not to accept any changes to the specifications without my knowledge. If a specification change was requested by the customer over the telephone, it did not matter how minor the change request was, it had to go through me. We all agreed to the new strict specification change rules. I revised the specifications to revision B and sent it to my customer's project manager for his approval.

Then I asked my customer's project manager to travel to our plant so that we could finalize the revised technical specifications. I sat with him for three days face-to-face to go over each redline and got his final approval for revision B to the contract's technical specifications. I told him that we were falling behind in the project due to the minor changes that were piling up. I asked him politely to go through all the changes with me whether they were minor or not. I told him he could talk to the individual design engineers as many times as he wished, but if there was a change looming on the horizon, he had to go through me. I emphasized that if the change was urgent, I could redline the technical specifications, sign it, and release it to the responsible design engineer that same day. Then I could have the technical specifications go through an official revision after piling up a couple of minor changes. If a change were going to affect the project schedule and cost, then I would provide him with my new schedule and cost estimates. I then could get the change approved and implemented only after his written concurrence with me regarding the new project schedule and project cost. He agreed with me on all my scope change procedures.

I kept the project technical specifications current. I made sure that changes went through our document control with top priority. I always kept my design engineers on top of the technical specifications. I reviewed all the changes during our weekly team meetings. When the project design phase was completed after nine months, the technical specifications were at revision K.

Similar technical specification control rules apply between your subcontractors and your company. Your customer should not be able to go to your subcontractor directly and ask for a scope change.

Technical specifications make up one of the critical legs of a project structure. The other three critical legs of the project structure are the schedule, the cost, and the team. If one of those legs is out of sync, the project will start to wobble, lose control, and sink. As project managers, we will definitely fail. Keeping the scope changes of a project under tight control without causing your customer to become frustrated and angry is a must.

LESSONS LEARNED FROM THIS PROJECT EVENT

- Taking on a project in the middle of execution is very courageous and risky.
- You have to absorb and evaluate all aspects of your new project very fast.
- You have to initiate changes to project activities that you see as inappropriate.
- It is always quite challenging to be able to change old established habits in a project environment.

Case 2.7: Bartering Minor Scope Changes

In a project, scope changes are a fact of life. Every time there is a scope change initiated by your customer, by yourself, and/or by your subcontractors, you do not have the luxury of going through several approval signatures and specification revisions. As a project manager, you have to assess if a scope change affects your project's cost, schedule, and team members. For minor effects, you do not have to rattle the apple cart and go through a tedious approval cycle and specification revisions. Many times, minor scope changes can be agreed upon between two project managers. You can receive an e-mail from your customer's project manager for his approval of a minor change you proposed or vice versa. You have to store these e-mails in case a conflict arises in the future.

I had several projects where minor scope changes occurred. I went along with my customer's requests without going through the mind-boggling change approval cycle. My customer's project manager followed a similar process. I applied similar rules to my subcontractors. I had to be practical. I bartered minor scope changes with my customers and with my subcontractors. For some picky customers' project managers, I collected all minor scope changes during the course of the project and revised all contract specifications at the closure of the project.

One example of bartering minor scope changes occurred during the design and construction of the equipment of an offshore oil platform. The control panel window size was specified as 10″ by 16″ with no tolerances. In the final design, our control panel window size came out to 9.5″ by 15″. I asked my customer's project manager for a deviation. He accepted and confirmed the new control panel window size by e-mail. He told me that he was going to ask me for a minor change too. The customer specification asked for a ¼-inch thick tempered glass cover for the equipment gauge panel. The customer's engineers wanted to change from glass material to Lexan polycarbonate with a UV-resistant exterior surface. Also, Lexan offered 250× the impact resistance of tempered glass at half the weight. I told him that I would investigate his change offer and get back to him in two days. We had already bought the tempered glass for the project. I called the glass vendor and discussed the material change in our design. He said that he would accept the return of the glass and only charge us a restocking fee, which was a small amount. I then called the Lexan vendor and got pricing and delivery information for the amount needed for the project. The delivery time was acceptable and the pricing was 6% higher. All these changes caused by the new material were minor and acceptable from my point of view. I called my customer's project manager and explained in detail the material change process. I bartered his scope change and sent him an acceptance e-mail. We did not go through a formal specification revision at that time. We did the update on all project specifications at the end of the project.

In another project for an advanced electric bus design and construction, plastic hanging passenger straps and their plastic fasteners came from the vendor in a cobalt blue color. The customer's specification asked for a gray color. I did not have time to reject the straps and their fasteners. Lead time was an issue. I called my customer's project manager and explained the color difference and what it would take to change them. I had done some minor specification changes for him in the past without a fuss. So he owed me one. He accepted the new color and confirmed it by e-mail.

These kinds of minor scope changes frequently occur especially in software design and development. The customer's project manager requests several minor software specification changes almost every day. My team members will also ask me to ask our customer for some minor changes in software specifications daily. A gentleman's understanding between two project managers is a must for the project to flow smoothly and not to have to wait through several approval signature cycles and document control procedures for specification revisions. As the project manager, the bottom line is to document these bartered minor specification changes in order to avoid any conflicts downstream.

LESSONS LEARNED FROM THIS PROJECT EVENT

- Approval of project scope and specification changes can be very tedious and time consuming both at your company and at your customer's company.
- Minor scope and specification changes can be accomplished in writing between you and your customer's project manager without going through the formal scope change process.

Case 2.8: Keeping Up with Software Revisions

During the execution of a project, team members use several different types of software. We have to deal with internally and externally developed software. We have to deal with customers' and subcontractors' software. We have to make sure that the software is compatible and at the same revision levels. I have come across several issues with software during my project management career. I will cover four such cases in this section.

We had an internally developed magnetic recording head flying height calculator software. All of the design engineers on my team used this software. The developer of the software was a well-known scientist who worked in the company's research and development group. He was good at what he developed, but he was not meticulous in document controlling his software's revisions and updating his software's user manual. My team's design engineers were using different versions of the software and they were making errors. I had to take this sloppy situation under control. I went to the scientist's office and politely explained several issues we had with his software. He accepted that his revision release process was not perfect. He told me that he was a sloppy, but good scientist and not a disciplined revision controller. It was going to be hard to change his sloppy behavior at his level. So I offered to release new versions of his software and user manual on document control myself and to inform all users. I wanted everyone to be on the same page when they used his flying height calculator software. He agreed with my proposal. I took over releasing new versions and user manual updates. All user errors diminished. My design engineers had no issues using our internally developed flying height calculator software.

I was heading a team in an oil platform subsystem design, manufacturing, and installation project for the Russian Federation. I used MS Project's latest revision as my project management software. I presented our project's schedule and critical tasks to my customer during the customer kickoff meeting. Everything was fine and dandy. My customer's project manager asked me to send him by e-mail an updated project schedule with percentage completed task estimates every Monday. The problem was that they could not open my MS Project file and review my updated project schedule. My customer's company used different project management software, which was not compatible with MS Project. I offered to send him my weekly updates in a PDF format. He accepted my solution. Every week after updating my project's schedule, I had to convert it to the PDF format and e-mail to my customer that way.

In another project software case, a subcontractor was designing and manufacturing some trolleys for a transport system on an oil platform. My design engineers were using the most current release of AutoCad to design the transport system. My trolley subcontractor was using an old version of AutoCad. By the way,

AutoCad had 28 revisions from its first release in 1982 through 2014. The subcontractor sent us his AutoCad drawing files for trolleys so that my design engineer could interface them into the system drawings and verify that there were no issues. Several callouts and dimensions on the trolley drawings were transferred erroneously. My design engineer had to check each and every callout and dimension for the trolleys and correct several of them so that our system drawings were intact. Backward compatibility of software releases should be checked very thoroughly at all costs. There can be some hidden surprises in different software releases.

In an integrated circuit design case, my team's design engineers used Verilog, a hardware description language software. My engineers were trained at school and at work to use Verilog software to describe functionalities of the circuit. One of my German customers required us to use VHDL software for the integrated circuit design for them. They put this requirement into their technical specifications. I discussed this design software choice issue with my customer's project manager. He insisted that internally, his company only used VHDL software. That was the reason they put this requirement into their specifications. So as their subcontractor, my designers had to use the VHDL software. He did not budge at all in using the Verilog software. Our sales group missed this critical point when they signed the contract with our customer. Most experienced ASIC (application specific integrated circuit) designers could use both kinds of software, but my team's design engineers were fresh out of school and they were only trained in using the Verilog software. I had to scramble and get a training program going for the VHDL software. I had my six design engineers trained in VHDL software in a crash course in two weeks. They designed all parts of the circuit for my German customer in VHDL language. They were slow at the beginning of the project, but they became more efficient as the project progressed. At the end of the project, all my design engineers were very thankful to me for making them learn the VHDL software. They became efficient in both kinds of software, which was good for them and for my company.

The software used in a project has to be scrutinized very carefully. There can be many unforeseen conflicts and issues between customers, subcontractors, and internal users. Errors generated by using different software and different software releases can sink a project's schedule and cost performance.

LESSONS LEARNED FROM THIS PROJECT EVENT

- Software used during the execution of your project by your team members, by your customers, and by your subcontractors has to be compatible and has to be at the same revision levels.
- Internally developed software has to be released through your document control and the software's revision levels have to be the same across your company.

3

CASE STUDIES IN KNOWLEDGE MANAGEMENT

Knowledge management is the foundation of your project. Depth of knowledge in your team members to your subcontractors can sail smoothly or sink a project.

My subcontractor was designing and constructing trolleys with a 10-ton load capacity for one of my projects. Contract specifications called for a bronze coating over the trolley wheels for a nonspark operation with very tight tolerances. My subcontractor insisted that a bronze coating with such tight tolerances was not manufacturable. He had to educate me on bronze coating techniques. He had to show me what was doable and what the limits of the bronze coating process were. I was a bridge between my subcontractor and my customer in order to get tight specifications relaxed. Details of this case are provided in Case 3.1.

My project management experience spanned several different technology-based companies. Leading-edge technical knowledge is the basis of an engineering project. I made sure that my engineers were trained and excelled in state of the art technological advances. When we bid for a project contract, we sold our technical knowledge and expertise in that particular field. I had to orchestrate to have an excellent collective technical knowledge internally and through our partners and consultants as depicted in Case 3.2.

As project managers, we have to make sure that all our team players are ready and up to par for presentations in front of the customers, regulatory agencies, inspectors, and upper management. Many factors can spoil a presentation as shown in Case 3.3.

As project managers, we should always encourage our project team members to record their new ideas and findings in engineering books and have them signed and dated by a colleague so that their new ideas and findings can be verified and patented for the company's and their benefit. An interesting patent application is described in Case 3.4.

The "not invented here" syndrome can happen at an individual level or at a company level. Some company officers sometimes refuse to change company designs or procedures by better and proven ones available from the outside. This organizational level of not invented here syndrome can degrade a company's performance and affect your project's performance as shown in Case 3.5.

As project managers, we have to encourage our team members to attend technical conferences and shows as long as they are within our company's guidelines. However, we have to establish with our team members as to who is going where at the beginning of the project. It is our responsibility to balance our project's responsibilities with technical conferences and shows as detailed in Case 3.6.

Methods of interpretation for a callout on a drawing can be quite different even from person to person in a global project as depicted in Case 3.7. Inviting the final user of the design drawings to the design review meeting is a must. As project managers, it is our responsibility to bridge the gap between the designer and the user.

Paying attention to details and checking out all possible consequences of a task is the first amendment in the laws of global engineering project management. In one of my global projects, I made a mistake in believing a departed project manager and my team's engineers regarding the equivalence of U.S. and European certification standards as detailed in Case 3.8.

Some project managers are closed-minded. They are intolerant and unreceptive to others' new ideas. Their actions discourage team members. Team members stop contributing for the good of the project. Even some out-of-line suggestions can have value. As project managers, we should listen to and weigh all options before deciding on a course of action in a task as depicted in Case 3.9.

As a global team, your team members should be knowledgeable of all pertinent project specifications and requirements. They have to trickle down as required to all the people involved in your global project as depicted in Case 3.10. In a global project, a personalized trickle down project management is not possible. In such cases, you have to rely on your offshore managers.

Intellectual property guidelines have to be sorted out at the beginning of a project. Do's and don'ts have to be advised to all team members. As project managers, we are totally responsible for honoring the intellectual property rules of a project. My several challenging encounters to protect intellectual property are given in Case 3.11.

Case 3.1: Respecifying Bronze Coating Thickness on Wheels

In project management, you are constantly destined to negotiate contract specifications with your customer and with your subcontractors. You start the project with clarified and agreed upon specifications during the bidding phase of the project. Most of these bidding phase deals might be done by the sales group of your company. When you get into the execution phase of the project you might realize that some of the specifications are not doable. You have to inform you customer's contract manager immediately and come to terms with him or her.

I had several heated negotiations with my customer's project manager about specifications during the design, construction, and installation of an offshore oil platform system. The design was for a Class 1 hazardous environment in which flammable gases or vapors could be present in the air in sufficient quantities to be explosive or ignitable. According to the contract specifications, all moving part surfaces had to be nonsparking.

One of my subcontractors was designing and constructing trolleys with a 10-ton load capacity. Contract specifications called for a $0.010'' \pm 0.001''$ thick bronze coating over the wheels for a nonspark operation. My subcontractor called me one morning and told me that his man, a sub-subcontractor, said that doing the bronze coating would not control the $\pm 0.001''$ thickness tolerance all the way around the wheel, especially at the radius between the bottom of the wheel and the sides of the wheel. He said that he talked with several other bronze coating people and received the same response. The best bronze thickness tolerance they could do around the radius was $\pm 0.005''$. He asked me to authorize a specification deviation for bronze coating tolerance over the radius of the wheels. I told him that I would contact my customer immediately and get back to him with a written specification deviation in a day.

I called my customer's project manager and explained the situation. He had to discuss the bronze coating tolerance issue with his engineer. I received a response from him in the afternoon that they could not relax the tolerance around the radius because of the Class 1 hazardous environment. His response was not acceptable. I had to pursue this specification relaxation so that my subcontractor could get the trolley wheels built. Wheel radius was a noncontact area and it did not touch the rails at all for spark generation. I asked him if I could discuss the tolerance relaxation issue directly with his engineer. He gave me permission to do so.

I called the mechanical engineer who put together the trolley specifications. He was a novice engineer right out of college. He was very adamant about the bronze coating tolerance specifications. I told him that no manufacturer in the United States could comply with his tight specifications around the radius of the trolley wheels. I assured him and showed him on our assembly drawings that there was no contact at the surface of the radius with the rails where I was requesting the relaxation of the bronze coating tolerance. I proposed to perform a 100% inspection for bronze coating thickness and for pinholes in coating around the radius. He felt better after I threw in the 100% inspection requirement and agreed to relax the specification. He informed my customer's project manager about his change of mind after the discussion with me and after my proposed 100% inspection requirement.

I received an e-mail confirming the bronze coating thickness relaxation around the radius to be 0.010″ ± 0.005″ with the 100% inspection requirement in the radius region. I forwarded to my subcontractor the relaxed specification. He was happy for the specification relaxation, but not happy about the added inspection. He told me that the 100% inspection was going to cost him four hours of extra inspection time for every trolley. I convinced him that you win some and you lose some in these specification negotiations. In this case, we won a more significant victory. The added burden of four hours of inspection per trolley was minor as compared to the bronze coating thickness relaxation in a hazardous environment.

LESSONS LEARNED FROM THIS PROJECT EVENT

- As project managers, we are the conduit connecting our subcontractors and our customers.
- You can learn a lot from your subcontractor about his special area of expertise.
- You have to evaluate your subcontractors' change requests in a timely fashion and help them to progress smoothly in their portions of the project.

Case 3.2: Technical Training Needs

My project management experience spanned several different technology-based companies. Leading-edge knowledge was the basis of our strength. I had to make sure that my engineers were trained and excelled in state of the art technological advances. When we bid for a project contract, we sold our knowledge and expertise in that particular field. I had to orchestrate collective technical knowledge internally and through our partners and consultants.

I was managing a project for an oil company in the Arctic region where the temperature plummeted down to −50°C. We had to perform our stress analyses of structures for 100-year seismic events at very low temperatures. I had four mechanical design engineers on my project team. Two of them needed to come up to speed in the latest developments in very low temperature stress analysis. I asked these two engineers to search and come up with a training plan for their upcoming tasks.

One of the design engineers came back to me with an extensive proposal. He wanted to take two classes and attend two conferences during the first three months of the project. He wanted to take a course online entitled, Fracture Toughness of Materials Crack Tip Displacement Theory at Very Low Temperatures. Another course he wanted to take at a local university was entitled, Alternating Stress Fatigue Analysis at Very Low Temperature. He wanted to attend two conferences. One was the Offshore Technology Conference and the other was the Mechanics of Time-Dependent Materials Conference. These courses and conferences were very good ones for our technology base, but that he would have to spend 20% of his time during the first six months of the project on training. Also, our company's overhead budget allowed for only one course and one conference expense per engineer every year.

I went to his cubicle and discussed his training proposal. I told him that I was very much in favor of getting training in leading-edge technologies. I also emphasized that my project's schedule and our company's education budget could not handle two courses and two conferences in the next six months. I asked him to prioritize his choices and take one course this year and the second course next year and to make similar choices in attending conferences. He agreed with me and decided on his course and conference choices for the first year. I took his choices to his supervisor and to human resources for their approval. Everything worked out so that my project was not delayed and one of my mechanical design engineers was trained appropriately.

The second mechanical design engineer on my team had a different view on technology training. Online courses that he chose were in game theory and in statistical process controls. He also wanted to attend the International Conference on Ocean, Offshore and Arctic Engineering in Oslo, Norway. I discussed his course and conference choices with him. His main interests were in mathematics. His game theory course choice did not apply to our technology base at all. His statistical process control choice applied only to our volume production products. His choice of a conference in Oslo, Norway, was going to be way over the allocated budget. I encouraged him to take courses more in line with our technology base. I also encouraged him to find an appropriate conference closer to home. He did more searching and came back to me with an online course in dynamic finite element analysis at very low temperatures. He switched his conference to an international pipeline conference in Houston, Texas. Both of his choices were approved by his supervisor and by our human resources department.

Orchestrating the technical knowledge base of a company is one of the most important and challenging tasks of a project manager. Learning gives impetus and constant drive to your team members. You have to have that flame for learning desire always lit in your team. Broad-based technological findings come out of collaborative efforts between your team members, your company departments, your consultants, your subcontractors, and your customers. Including the needed courses and conferences into your project schedule for every team member should be one of your top priorities.

LESSONS LEARNED FROM THIS PROJECT EVENT

- Keeping your local and international team members up to speed with advancing technology should be top priority for an engineering project manager.
- Necessary training courses and conferences should be included in your project's schedule and budget.

Case 3.3: Abysmal Performance at Design Review

I had an excellent group of five software design engineers in a one-year project to upgrade a data communication chip. My customer was U.S. based. The project was moving smoothly on schedule and within budget. I was updating my customer's project manager by telephone weekly and was sending him a weekly document controlled progress report.

We were scheduled to have our first design review meeting in two weeks at our facilities. My customer's project manager, their engineering vice president, and their two senior engineers were going to attend the design review meeting. I arranged for our internal design review meeting one week before the one with the customer. First, I gave an overall status of the project. Then each of my software design engineers summarized their portions of the project. After each presentation, I opened the floor for questions and answers. Some engineers needed some polishing in critical areas, especially related to complying with the customer's specifications. Overall, we were ready for the big day facing the customer the following week.

The design review meeting started with initial introductions and with small talk regarding the data communications industry. My customer's engineering vice president emphasized the importance of the chip we were designing for his company and how it fit into their future product plan. Then I presented the overall status of the project. I detailed the schedule and cost performance indices for each task group. Afterward, my two software design engineers presented the status of their tasks. There were several discussions regarding the specifications and their clarifications. Everything was going according to my plan and my customer seemed very relaxed and happy about the progress of the project. Afterward we had a lunch break. Lunch was brought into the conference room. After a quick bite to eat, everyone rushed to check their e-mails and respond to their voice mails. I reserved two offices for my customer's people so that they could work in privacy during their breaks in our facilities.

After lunch, the third software design engineer from my team began his presentation. He started to deviate from his prepared PowerPoint presentation and then stumbled over several specification clarification questions. I tried to intervene and correct the situation. My software design engineer seemed to be in another world. I was worried. I immediately asked for a recess. I took the software design engineer to my office to find out what was happening to him. He started crying. He told me that he had a fight at home with his wife. She was going to leave him. He could not sleep all night. He was devastated. I told him that he should have informed me before the meeting as to what was going on with him. I could have canceled his presentation. He told me that he had thought he could still perform well under his highly stressed condition. He was very sorry that he botched his presentation in front of the customer. I told him to go home, to get some rest, and to straighten himself out. I told him that I would take care of the customer and would explain his situation to them.

We reconvened in the conference room after a half an hour break. I explained to my customer that my software design engineer had a family issue and he was highly stressed out. He could not continue his presentation. I also told them that my software design engineer was good and reliable. I offered to visit their facilities with my software design engineer and he could give his portion of the presentation as soon as he straightened out his family issues. They agreed to my proposal and they wished a speedy recovery to my software design engineer. The rest of the design review meeting went well. They said that they would release the partial project payment to my company after we had completed the design review at their facilities. I informed upper management and our human resources of what had happened, but I assured them that everything was under control and my software design engineer was an excellent talent for our company.

Two weeks after the eventful design review meeting, my software design engineer settled down. He straightened out his family issues and he was back to normal. He again apologized to me and to all the team members during our weekly team meeting. I arranged for the continuation of our design review meeting at our customer's place. He made a good presentation there and our customer was very satisfied with his much-improved performance. I fully supported my software design engineer during his unfortunate ordeal. The only setback was the two weeks of delay for our partial payment.

After this episode, I made sure beforehand that all my team players were up to par for presentations in front of the customers, regulatory agencies, inspectors, upper management, and so on.

LESSONS LEARNED FROM THIS PROJECT EVENT

- A project manager has to prepare his or her team members meticulously for project design review meetings with customers.
- If something goes haywire during a project design review meeting with your customer, immediately request a recess to correct the issue at hand.
- Right before design review meetings, make sure that all your team members are in top-notch condition to give their presentations.

Case 3.4: Patent Rights

In the computer disk drive industry, the cost of the drives decreased every year while the areal density of the information that was recorded on a magnetic disk increased exponentially. We had to keep ahead of our competition. There was no breathing room to pause or relax for a moment. I was heading a team of magnetic design engineers to improve the performance of our magnetic recording heads. My team came up with several ideas to advance the magnetic recording process. One such idea was to reshape the magnetic head slider so that it could fly closer to the magnetic disk and also it could be shaped so that magnetic flux losses in the slider body could be minimized. This idea came from one of my senior physicists.

I always cautioned my engineers to write down their findings in their engineering books and have them signed and dated by a colleague. When the patent application time came for an improved design, being detailed in your engineering write-ups, and signatures and dates was very important. The improved magnetic head design idea had to be verified. Two engineers on my team and the senior physicist got a couple of thousand magnetic heads made to the new design and got them tested thoroughly for a month. We saw statistically significant improvements in the magnetic head performance. We were elated and I immediately called our company's patent lawyer for a patent application.

We kept the information about our improved magnetic head design within our team and the patent lawyer until the patent was officially applied for to the U.S. patent office. We wanted to protect our intellectual property overseas too, especially in the disk drive manufacturing centers such as Japan, Malaysia, and Singapore. We also applied for a patent in those countries.

The senior physicist and the two engineers sat down with the patent lawyer for a week and detailed the present invention. At the same time they detailed the prior art in the magnetic recording field. They put together 11 drawings to describe the preferred embodiment. They summarized the improved test results of the new invention as compared to current day magnetic recording heads. Then they formulated the claims, all 43 of them. Claims were the most important portion of the patent application. It had a layer-by-layer structure starting with the basic claim and then expanding the basic claim to cover all possible variations to the basic claim.

Our patent lawyer went through a couple of revisions before finalizing the patent application. He called me after a week and told me that he was ready to submit the patent application, but the senior physicist wanted to have his name as the only inventor on the patent application. I was very surprised at this development because the two engineers on my team and the physicist worked together for a month to verify the proposed invention. Then they all wrote portions of the patent as a team with our patent lawyer. The invention was the senior physicist's idea, but without experimental verification his idea was worthless.

I called the senior physicist to my office and expressed to him how proud I was of their new invention. I told him that our company was going to benefit a lot from the improved magnetic recording head. Once the patent application process was completed, we were going to announce the improved magnetic recording head to our customers and at industry shows and conferences. I told him that all this would not have been possible if all three of them did not work diligently for a month as a team and verified his idea. He argued with me that the improved magnetic recording head was his idea. I emphasized that ideas are not patentable, but inventions were. In order for his idea to be an invention we had to go through a tedious test process. We had to show that his idea resulted in a substantial magnetic head performance.

My senior physicist finally agreed to my logic and agreed to include the other two engineers' names on the inventors list. The patent assignee was our company. After the patent application, we announced our advanced magnetic recording head to the world. Within a year, it became the main component in several disk drives. My senior physicist and my two engineers were given company appreciation plaques at a banquet for their patent. They were also handsomely rewarded during the annual bonus distributions.

I have always encouraged my project team members to record their new ideas and findings in engineering books and to have them signed and dated by a colleague so that their new ideas and findings could be verified and patented for the company's and their benefit.

LESSONS LEARNED FROM THIS PROJECT EVENT

- All contributors should share names on a patentable invention.
- As project managers, we have to encourage and guide our team members to apply for patents.

- Patents increase the value of your company and give your team members pride and an extra spark to create fresh and leading-edge inventions.
- Processing patent applications in foreign countries can take a long time and they can be expensive. You have to choose countries for patent application very carefully.

Case 3.5: Not Invented Here Factor

I had on my team a senior mechanical designer who was an expert in vehicle structural design. He designed vehicle structures during his engineering career for 20 years. He always resisted ideas or input from his teammates and from external sources. He had an extreme case of not invented here syndrome. When we were developing a light vehicle frame for our project, he never considered using advanced technology materials in his designs such as plastics, aluminum, high-strength steels, and so forth, as suggested by others.

I had extensive discussions with him regarding advances in vehicles. I encouraged him regularly to interact with a wider vehicle design community, to read related journals and to go to pertinent conferences. He had high self-esteem and self-confidence. He was a good engineer, but he had an attitude that if he did not invent or design a vehicle's structural component it would be inferior to what he would have come up with. His was a very counterproductive behavior. Vehicle and materials technology were advancing with lightning speed. If he looked around and listened to his colleagues he did not have to reinvent the wheel.

I had to address his not invented here factor and remedy it. His behavior was causing our vehicle design to be inferior to our competitors' designs. I could not rotate him to other tasks on my team. He was the only player in his field in our company. I could not fire him because he was a successful engineer. He was very good at what he produced. I had to remove him from his enclosed pedestal and make him consider all feasible design options. I started challenging him with fresh design perspectives and asked him to look into them during our weekly one-on-one meetings. I forced him to go to pertinent technical conferences. I asked several well-known vehicle structure design consultants to attend our design review meetings. He started to listen to our consultants' reviews. That was encouraging, but I had to bring him into a new way of global thinking.

Then I went a step further to remedy his syndrome and asked a vehicle structure design consultant to generate an independent design within the given parameters in order to create a design competition. This design competition idea increased my project's budget by 5%. I explained my design and personnel issues to my management and received their approval to go ahead with a second design.

During the final design review meeting with our customer, I had both designs presented. Our customer preferred our consultant's design to my senior mechanical designer's design. The consultant's design was more on par with the advanced vehicle structural design concepts. The consultant's vehicle structural design used more plastics and it was lighter in weight, but a little more expensive to manufacture than the senior mechanical engineer's design. This design competition and his design's defeat really opened my senior mechanical design engineer's eyes.

My senior mechanical design engineer came to my office the next day and discussed his status in our company. He was very humbled. He was afraid that he was going to be fired since he lost the design competition. I assured him that his notions were erroneous. I praised him as an engineer, but I reiterated that he had to open his eyes to the outside world, soften his perception of superiority, and utilize advances made by others. He thanked me for initiating the design competition. He said that he learned a lot from the consultant's design. He was apologetic for his counterproductive behavior in the past.

The not invented here syndrome can happen at an individual level or at a company level. Some company officers sometimes refuse to change company designs or procedures by better and proven ones available from the outside. This organizational level not invented here syndrome can degrade a company's performance. Correcting such cases might require significant organizational restructuring.

LESSONS LEARNED FROM THIS PROJECT EVENT

- It takes quite an effort to open the minds of some seasoned and specialized engineers.
- As project managers, we have to be open-minded and prevent not invented here syndrome among our team members and even within our company structure.

Case 3.6: A Technical Conference Conflicts with a Project's Progress

Technical conferences and shows are a part of an engineer's working life. He or she has to attend all pertinent events that would help to stay in touch and to compete in his or her field of expertise. I always encouraged my team members to go to technical conferences and shows as long as they were planned well ahead of time and they were accounted for in the project's schedule. All companies that I worked for had well-defined rules, procedures, and budgets for attending technical conferences and shows. If you were making a presentation at a session, you always got priority to attend. If you already attended a certain conference or a show the year before, management would give priority to someone else in your field the following year. If you had a critical deadline or an event at the company, you had to forgo the week at the conference or at the show. Sometimes there were company cash flow issues, which restricted travel expenses and the number of attendees to technical conferences and shows. I remember going to one conference on my own dime.

During my career, I came across several surprising occurrences to my team members regarding technical conferences and shows. All these surprising occurrences affected the progress of my project at that time. In one such case, four out of eight engineers working for me on a yearlong project came to my office one day with smiling faces and informed me that they had gotten approval from their managers to attend the Comdex show the following week, a computer exposition show that occurred annually in Las Vegas. I was dumbfounded. I told them that they should have first consulted me before approaching their managers. My project was in a crunch time. All they thought about was a fun week at Comdex in Las Vegas. They forgot all about their responsibilities to my project. I did not want to put my weight down, cancel their attendance to Comdex, and disappoint them. We had to find a solution together. I went over each engineer's tasks. If three of the engineers worked 60 hours per week for two weeks after the show, they could catch up to the project's schedule and would not cause any harm. So three of the engineers were okay to go, but one test engineer had to perform crucial training for two Malaysian engineers during the week of the show. The Malaysian engineers were already at our plant and they were scheduled to fly back to their country immediately after the training. I had another test engineer on my team. I decided to bring him into our meeting too to see if he could help us out of the bind we were in. We went over the training tasks one by one. The other test engineer agreed to take over the following week's training tasks. He agreed to work an extra 20 hours the following week so that his teammate could attend Comdex. That was good camaraderie in a project environment. I agreed to let four engineers attend Comdex the following week. I advised them to approach such a technical conference or show requests in the future in a timely fashion by considering all of their project responsibilities.

Another surprise came from an urgent replacement presenter at the IEEE (Institute of Electrical and Electronics Engineers) annual conference of industrial electronics in Europe. A physicist at our company became ill and could not fly on an airplane to Europe. My upper management decided to send a replacement. The upper management decided to send one of my team members without consulting me or my team member. The vice president of engineering called me and my team member to his office and explained the need for the replacement presenter at the upcoming conference in three days. According to my upper management, my team member was the best-qualified replacement presenter in our company. What could I say? What could my team member say? We could not object to such an emergency request. I told the vice president that I was going to sit down with my team member and find a way to get him to go to the conference in Europe in three days without affecting his duties on my project. I had to take over my team member's project responsibilities for the next 10 days. I heard that he did a great job as the replacement presenter at the conference in Europe and my project had a minor setback.

A strange case happened regarding a Consumer Electronics Show (CES). Apparently, a project team member of mine was a regular attendee at this annual show. He thought that one week every year at CES was a given to him by our company. He did not even bother to inform me about his CES attendance at the beginning of the project. I scheduled a critical design review meeting with our customer, which unfortunately coincided with the CES week. He came to my office a couple of weeks before the show and told me that he made his arrangements to attend the CES. I was quite surprised. I told him that we were going to have a critical design review during that week with our customer and he had to be present at that meeting. I insisted that everything was set up with our customer and he could not go to the CES. He had to cancel all arrangements that he had made for the show. He was very upset, left my office, and went to his supervisor to complain. His supervisor called me to discuss the conflict. After I explained the details of the case, his supervisor agreed with me that critical design review took priority and canceled his engineer's trip to CES. It was an unfortunate coincidence, but if he had declared his plans to me at the beginning of the project, then I could have scheduled the critical design review accordingly.

As project managers, we have to encourage our team members to attend technical conferences and shows as long as they are within our company's guidelines. However, we have to establish with our team members who is going where at the beginning of the project. It is our responsibility to balance our project's responsibilities with technical conferences and shows.

LESSONS LEARNED FROM THIS PROJECT EVENT

- Every team member's schedule for attending technical conferences and shows should be on our project schedule from the start.
- We, as project managers, have to balance fairly an engineer's wish to attend a technical conference and/or a show with his or her project responsibilities.

Case 3.7: Redimensioning of Design Drawings

Generating design drawings for a project can be very tricky sometimes. If the construction of the parts will be done in Europe, it is advisable to use ISO 128-21 standards. If the construction of parts will be done in the United States, it is advisable to use ASME 14.5 standards. If you study both standards, they look similar, but there are many subtle differences. A machinist in Europe can misinterpret concentricity, symmetry, and so on, callouts on a drawing that is dimensioned according to ASME 14.5 standards, since they are trained and use drawings constructed according to ISO 128-21.

In one of my projects we were designing several large and thick steel plates with precision holes and slots to be used on an oil platform. My engineers were trained in geometric dimensioning and tolerancing per ASME 14.5 standards. We completed the design drawings for the steel plates and our purchasing department solicited bids domestically and internationally to build 20 steel plates. Our purchasing department found the best deal with a French company and subcontracted them to build the steel plates. In the past, this French company had a good track record with our company for building complicated steel structures.

Our purchasing agent and I started to have weekly teleconferences with the French subcontractor. During the first call, they asked us to update our drawings to relocate the datum reference planes, since their large milling machines could not locate the precision holes and slots from the ones on the drawings. We immediately updated four drawings, released them through document control, and e-mailed them in four days. The French subcontractor started to machine the first article. During our teleconferences, they assured me that there were no other issues with dimensioning and tolerancing of our drawings.

Two weeks passed and they were ready for the first article acceptance. I sent one of my quality engineers to France for the first article acceptance. During the first article acceptance measurements, my quality engineer discovered that the symmetry of the holes was out of tolerance for what was called out on the drawings. The French machinist misunderstood the symmetry tolerancing in the ASME Y14.5 standard. My quality engineer had to reject the first article. Luckily, I had a design engineer on my team who was also trained in ISO 128-21 standards. I asked him to update all four drawings again. This time he made sure that all the dimensions and tolerances were called out per ISO 128-21. I e-mailed the new revised drawings to France. They rebuilt the first article. I sent my quality engineer to France again. The French subcontractor passed the first article dimensional inspection with flying colors the second time around. Finally, we got our French subcontractor to build correctly our 20 large and thick steel plates with precision holes and slots. The plates were delayed three weeks for delivery. Fortunately, completion of the plates was not on the critical path of the whole project.

In a global industry, as the project manager, you have to be cognizant of the standards and procedures that are used in that particular country. This applies to dimensioning and tolerances, to certifications, to material origins, to machines used for certain processes, quality control practices, and so on. You would be surprised to find vast differences from country to country.

What I should have done was to have the French machinist review all four drawings for every dimension and tolerance during a teleconference. I had to make sure that he was on the same page as my design engineer. Then I should have asked our purchasing department to reword the contract.

Methods of interpretation for a callout on a drawing can be quite different even from person to person in a global project. Inviting the final user of the design drawings to the design review meeting is a must. As a project manager, it was my responsibility to bridge the gap between the designer and the user.

LESSONS LEARNED FROM THIS PROJECT EVENT

- Your design drawings and user manuals have to be user-friendly in a global project environment. Users in foreign countries have to be able to understand and be able to interpret them easily.
- Always invite final users of your design drawings and user manuals to your design review meetings.

Case 3.8: Component Certification

I took on a project in the middle of the design phase because the original project manager was leaving the company. The project was to design and build control consoles for a hazardous environment with combustible gases and vapors. Our customer was in Europe. The departing project manager and I had five days of overlapping period so that he could bring me up to date on all significant aspects of the project. The departing project manager introduced me to every member of my new team. There were five engineers in the group. They were all experienced in their specialties. The departing project manager, our customer's project manager, and I had a two-hour videoconference in order to make a seamless transfer of responsibilities. The departing project engineer went over all the critical specifications with me. He briefed me on the schedule, cost structure, and status. Everything seemed to be in order and progressing smoothly.

All electrical components, enclosures, and assemblies had to be certified for a Class 1 and Division 1 hazardous area environment. Electrical control enclosures were going to be used outdoors. They had to be protected against corrosion, windblown dust and rain, splashing water, and ice formation. The departing project manager assured me that as long as the control enclosures were NEMA 4X (U.S. National Electrical Manufacturers Association) certified, we did not have to get recertification according to the European standards, namely IP56 (ingress protection rating in Europe).

My team completed the design on time. We bought components that were certified both in the United States and in Europe for a Class 1 and Division 1 hazardous area environment. The European certification standards were written by IEC, Electrotechnical Commission International. The only issue arose in the electrical control enclosures. One of the assemblers notified me that the control enclosures were only NEMA 4X certified. I called the control enclosure's manufacturer and talked to them about the European IP56 certification of their product. They told me not to worry because both NEMA 4X and IP56 certifications were equivalent. I received the same response from my team's engineers.

My last stop was our customer's project manager. I called him and asked him the same certification question about electrical control enclosures. He cautioned me that both hazardous area standards were very similar, but our contract called for certification of all electrical components, enclosures, and assemblies according to European Union IP56 standards. He would not budge on the electrical control enclosures certification. We had to return all 15 control enclosures back to their manufacturer with a minimum of cost penalty. I mobilized our purchasing department and my team's engineers to source 15 control enclosures that complied with our design and that were certified in Europe. Delivery time was also an issue. We had to have these control enclosures in three weeks time in order to meet our schedule. I asked our customer's project manager for his suggested sources too. He could not be of much help.

After a week of frantic searching, we finally found a small electrical control enclosure manufacturer in Germany who was willing to build and test for us 15 control enclosures according to our design and to the European hazardous area standard IP56. This was quite a relief to me and to my team. I had to pay extra for transportation to get them airfreighted to the United States on a priority basis. In the end, we were delayed a week in delivering of our product, which complied completely with the European hazardous area standards including assemblies. I had to send a 400-page binder of compliance certificates to our customer along with our deliverables.

It was my mistake to believe the departed project manager and my engineers regarding the equivalence of U.S. and European certification standards. I should have emphasized that all components and enclosures were to be checked for IP56 standard certificates at receiving inspection. There were some minor differences, but the bottom line was my customer's specification, which required that all electrical components, enclosures, and assemblies had to be certified for a Class 1 and Division 1 hazardous area environment according to the IP56 standard.

LESSONS LEARNED FROM THIS PROJECT EVENT

- Taking on a project in the middle of execution can be very tricky. You have to have a long enough transition period so that the project management transfer is seamless.
- Certification standards in other countries can have slight differences from the ones we have in the United States.

Case 3.9: A Practical Solution to Fluid Flow Simulation

I was a senior scientist on a team that designed and built a rotary combustion engine for passenger vehicles. Our team was struggling to optimize the design of engine housing coolant flow deflectors. These flow deflectors gave direction and increased turbulent energy of the engine's water coolant and thereby increased convection heat transfer capability from combustion chambers. These flow deflectors had to prevent any stagnant flow regions, had to prevent cavitation, and had to prevent bubble formation on housing walls. Optimized flow deflectors decreased engine housing wall temperatures and therefore thermal stresses in the cast housing material.

We had several team meetings regarding the flow deflectors optimization approach. Our team's project manager wanted to use an advanced fluid flow simulation program that was going to be run for optimization by an expert consultant. Then we were going to verify the consultant's fluid flow simulation program results in a laboratory at a nearby university by building a clear plexiglass model of the engine housing with optimized flow deflectors. This approach was going to take three months and was going to be expensive for the project.

I proposed a simpler solution for the optimization. I told my team that we could build an engine housing model with several different flow deflectors from clear plexiglass and test them visually by running water at different flow rates through them. We could watch and take pictures to see if there were any stagnant flow regions. We could modify the flow deflectors easily and rerun the flow experiments until we found the optimum flow deflector design by trial and error. My trial and error experimental approach was going to take about one month and be one-quarter of the cost of the simulation program optimization efforts.

Our team's project manager insisted on using the simulation program optimization. He was determined in that approach from the beginning of the project. I discussed with him several times my trial and error experimental approach in the laboratory. He never listened to my quicker, cheaper, and simpler optimization suggestion. He was the leader of our team. We had to go along with his choice. The program manager contracted an expert consultant in fluid flow simulations. The consultant's simulation optimization took three months. Then we had to build a model of the engine housing with optimized flow deflectors and test it. Simulation optimization verification efforts took another two weeks. The results were very discouraging. There were two areas in the engine housing where the water flow stagnated. However, flow simulations showed normal turbulent flow in those two stagnant regions. We wasted three and a half months and a lot of the project's funds without success. We had to start the optimization process over again. This time, the project manager came to me and confessed that he should have listened to my proposal in the first place.

The project was delayed for no good reason. Our project manager was grilled by our upper management too. Upper management got the gist of my practical proposal for a flow deflectors design optimization and got after our project manager for refusing to go along with my proposal. They were definitely stressful times in our project.

We went back to optimizing the flow deflectors' design using the trial and error experimental method that I had outlined for the team. We had the engine housing model already. We only had to change deflector shapes and positions. After two weeks and 14 trials, we narrowed the deflectors' design to their optimized shapes and positions in the engine housing. At our team meeting, the project manager again thanked me for being practical and achieving such a quick solution to a difficult problem.

Listening to others and evaluating all of the input are the most important virtues of a good project manager. Some project managers are very closed-minded. They are intolerant and unreceptive of others' new ideas. Their actions discourage team members. Team members stop contributing for the good of the project. Even some out-of-line suggestions can have value. As project managers, we should listen to and weigh all options before deciding on a course of action.

LESSONS LEARNED FROM THIS PROJECT EVENT

- Some project managers are not good listeners and they want things done their way.
- As project team members, we should not get discouraged when a project manager shoots down our ideas. We should be empowered by our project's goals and keep providing constructive input to our team.

Case 3.10: Traceability of Heat Lot Numbers

I was the project manager for a two-year project involving component design, manufacturing, and installation for a new oil platform destined for the Gulf of Mexico. The project technical specifications and requirements were compiled into a 400-page handbook. The handbook contained the scope of the project, component performance criteria, classification, certification and regulation requirements, operational life requirements, fatigue life requirements, operation criteria, installation criteria, environmental criteria, transit conditions, corrosion protection and coating criteria, marking and tagging criteria, quality plan requirements, inspection requirements, testing requirements, design drawing and design calculations requirements, project management, reporting and scheduling requirements, dimensioning, weights and center of gravity requirements, shipping requirements, ship yard commissioning and preservation manual requirements, installation, operation and maintenance manual requirements, and certification data book requirements.

As the project manager, I had to absorb every word in that handbook and distribute the project's technical specifications and requirements to every pertinent team member. Some specifications and requirements were hidden in the layers of the handbook. For example, testing requirements were further broken up into functional tests, load tests, nondestructive tests, mechanical tests, electrical tests, and environmental tests.

As a team, we were able to deal with all of the specifications and requirements except one, namely, traceability of some raw materials to their origins. The project requirements required complete traceability of raw materials for steel plates, forgings, castings, fasteners, pins, and shafts from their original heat lots to finished products. We had to stamp the heat lot number and the vendor designation on the part. If we could not use stamping due to component size or due to an available surface, we had to tag the part with the traceability information. I warned our manufacturing manager about this traceability requirement at the beginning of the project. However, this project requirement information did not trickle down to our machinists. The machinists worked on the special steel to manufacture the required components for two months. After machining, all original heat lot information for the special steel pieces were lost. We could not tell which finished component came from which special steel heat lot. We purchased the special steel for the project from two different customer-approved steel vendors and according to our receiving inspection records they were produced in five different heat lots.

I called an urgent meeting with our manufacturing manager, receiving inspection manager, stockroom manager, and our six machinists. We brainstormed the issue at hand. The stockroom manager and our six machinists were very helpful. They came up with a good idea for how to trace the special steel back to its original heat lot. When a machinist requested a piece of the special steel from our stockroom, the stockroom personnel recorded the date, the heat lot information, vendor information, and the machinist who received it. By going back to these stockroom records, with the help of our machinists, we were able to determine where the original material came from for every finished component. The machinists had to remember when they built each part during the last two months. By using the elimination method, we were able to pin down every finished component's heat lot number and vendor. Every machinist stamped or tagged his own finished component. The manufacturing manager was very apologetic about missing a simple requirement for my project.

After this episode, I made sure that every project requirement detail was understood and complied with by the people who did the work. I discussed the project requirement with their managers, but more importantly with every one of them who did the work individually. This kind of personalized trickle down project management was not possible in a global project. In such cases, I used written e-mails and also I had to verbally remind the offshore managers several times to make sure that their people knew and complied with the applicable project requirements.

LESSONS LEARNED FROM THIS PROJECT EVENT

- A project's technical specification and requirements can be very complicated and tedious to understand. Some technical specifications and requirements can appear in several different customer documents and they can contradict each other.

- Every pertinent technical specification and requirement has to trickle down to its user on our team.
- As project managers, it is our responsibility to make sure that every technical specification and requirement is complied with during the execution of our projects.

Case 3.11: Protecting Intellectual Property

During the execution of a project intellectual property guidelines can be very complicated for a project manager to comprehend and to apply. Before the project begins, the project manager has to make sure that he understands all intricacies governing intellectual property under his project's umbrella. If he needs clarifications about intellectual property rules he immediately should seek help from his company's lawyers and from his customer's project manager. Patents, copyrights, trademarks, and secrecy rules governing his project should be crystal clear to a project manager before the execution of the project starts.

In an advanced automobile design project, my company had to defend at our cost, indemnify, and hold harmless our customer and my company against a liability suit that a component manufacturer opened against us. The lawsuit was for infringement of a patent that my team members and I had overlooked for using a component in contention for our design without the component manufacturer's permission and royalty payment. My company lost the case. That was an expensive lesson I experienced during my career. After that experience I was very careful to check all patents and pros and cons before using someone else's intellectual property in my projects.

In another intellectual property case, an engineer on my team wanted to apply for a patent. His new idea and design were a result of technical input from our customer. I told him that he could not apply for that patent because his invention was mainly based on technical information received from our customer. Therefore, according to our contract his invention was the property of our customer. I had to promptly notify my customer's project manager about his invention. After several discussions with my customer's project manager and his company's lawyers, we agreed to file a joint patent for the new invention as long as my company paid for the patent application expenses. My engineer, my customer, and my company were all satisfied with the final resolution.

In another intellectual property case, my company had to share my project team's inventions with my subcontractor's company. This subcontractor was crucial for our design. Before signing a contract with us, the subcontractor requested that we share all inventions that would result from our joint design. My company's lawyers, my subcontractor's lawyer, and I had several meetings on this issue. We were doing a substantial portion of the design. We negotiated that any inventions resulting from our design would be applied for jointly. However, royalties coming in from such patents would be split 80/20, namely, we were going to get a major share of all the royalties. We signed the contract. Four patents resulted from our joint design efforts. Both parties were satisfied with the shared intellectual property rights.

Protecting a customer's intellectual property can require extensive planning and can be very time consuming in some projects. In such a project, I had to form a team which was totally separated from my company's other duties. Everyone on my team was 100% dedicated to that secretive and advanced technology project. Even our offices were relocated to a remote corner of the company. Coded locks were put on the entrances to our offices. Only my team members and I could enter that remote area. All design drawings and personally assigned laptop computers were kept in a vault. Drawing copies were made only by receiving written permission from the customer's representative. I had to make sure that all drawings and laptop computers were safely in the vault before I left for the evening. We were sworn not to discuss technical details of that project with anyone outside of our team. The manufacturing side of that project was another nightmare. Whole manufacturing and test areas were isolated by opaque plastic walls. No one was allowed to enter those restricted areas except the operators and the engineers who worked for that secret project. We were constantly monitored by our customer's representatives. We had some minor security breaches during the two-year project. My team members and I were very happy when the project was completed. The whole project environment was like a high-security prison. However, it was a very lucrative project for my company. We were able to protect our customer's intellectual property with very detailed planning and control.

Intellectual property guidelines have to be sorted out at the beginning of a project. All of the team members should be advised about the do's and don'ts. As project managers, we are totally responsible for honoring the intellectual property rules of a project.

LESSONS LEARNED FROM THIS PROJECT EVENT

- As project managers, we are responsible for protecting the intellectual property of our company, our customers, and our subcontractors.
- At the beginning of a project, all intellectual property protection rules pertaining to our project have to be explained to our team members.
- Protecting intellectual property in a global project environment requires very tight controls.

4

CASE STUDIES IN SCHEDULE MANAGEMENT

Schedule performance management of a global project is very time consuming for a project manager. Unexpected delays at your subcontractors, at your suppliers, and in information flow can devastate your project's progress.

I got devastating news from our subcontractor that his special steel supplier in Germany delayed their delivery another four months due to a large order from China. The whole steel factory capacity was dedicated to China for several months and our subcontractor's small order was pushed out another four months, which impacted my project's schedule very unfavorably. I had to scramble to straighten out this issue in Case 4.1.

A French subcontractor in one of my projects informed me with regret that his machinists voted to strike and they did not accept my subcontractor's terms for the new contract. An uncertain delay in the subcontractor's delivery schedule surfaced. I had to scramble to find another resource to replace my subcontractor in the middle of my project as detailed in Case 4.2.

Managing a monster-size project schedule for a large project can be very tedious and time consuming. A project manager should break down the monster project schedule file into manageable major task groups and subcontractor groups. Then he or she should create a master project schedule that includes the results of major task groups, all critical document delivery dates to the customer, all internal and customer design review meetings, and the customer's acceptance test dates and payment milestones. I present a large such challenging project in Case 4.3.

Global projects such as the one detailed in Case 4.4 put a lot of excessive strain on a project manager. Precise time management in different time zones is the only way to smooth out and effectively monitor the progress of your project.

Critical path tasks need more attention and more detailed scrutinizing during the execution of a global project. Case 4.5 details changes and their impact on a critical path task that heavily impacted several of my global projects.

Estimating task completion percentages periodically can be very tricky in a global project as shown in Case 4.6. As global engineering project managers, it is our responsibility to determine task completion percentages as accurately as possible. Our schedule and cost performance can give false implications about the health of our projects to us and to our upper management.

Case 4.1: Material Delays in a Hydraulic Cylinder Manufacturer

I was assigned to a yearlong project to build automated heavy equipment movement systems for a Norwegian customer. Final testing and acceptance of the systems were to be in California. Then the systems were to be surface shipped to Malaysia for installation and usage. I had several critical subcontractors in the project. These subcontractors were controlled by our purchasing agents on a part-time basis and these purchasing agents reported to me for the project on a dotted line. A Dutch subcontractor had six months to complete 20 high-pressure hydraulic cylinders for the project and surface ship them to California. This Dutch subcontractor also had a good track record with our company for on-time and quality product delivery.

I let our purchasing agent control this subcontractor by calling them every two weeks and getting updates on the progress of the project. At the end of the second month, we learned that the special steel provider from Germany for the casings of the hydraulic cylinders would delay their delivery by a month. Our subcontractor assured us that even with this material delay he would complete the project on time. We accepted the one-month delay for the special steel delivery and the fabrication start-up. Our subcontractor had all other components and materials in house to start the fabrication.

Another month passed. We got devastating news from our subcontractor that their special steel supplier in Germany delayed the delivery another four months due to a large order from China.

The whole steel factory capacity was dedicated to China for several months and our subcontractor's small order was pushed out another four months. This push out of raw material was totally unacceptable. After several telephone conversations with our subcontractor, the best he could do was to deliver the completed and tested hydraulic cylinders by airfreight three months late to our facilities in California. This would delay the delivery of assembled, tested, customer-accepted, and airfreighted systems to our customer in Malaysia by two months. A two-month delay in the project would cause heavy liquidated damages and a black eye to my company. I raised the emergency flag immediately. I called an emergency upper management meeting to discuss the grim situation and to take the necessary steps to remedy the issue. I also invited the president of our subcontractor to join the meeting by teleconferencing.

I depended totally on this subcontractor who had an excellent track record and I did not put in more rigorous controls to monitor their progress and to understand in detail the risks they were taking. I prepared for the emergency upper management/subcontractor meeting the next day. I put together several options to remedy the issue. I prepared a risk analysis and cost benefit analysis for each option.

The first order of business was to take full control of the situation and not depend on the subcontractor. I was given full responsibility to establish such control over this subcontractor. The company provided the purchasing agent in charge of the subcontractor to report to me on a full-time basis. I also requested a full-time quality engineer by name. I sent him to the Netherlands after getting the Dutch subcontractor's permission to monitor the subcontractor on location.

One option was to find another hydraulic cylinder manufacturer who had the special steel material in stock and cancel the contract with the Dutch subcontractor. This option was dropped during the meeting because the hydraulic cylinder design was already completed by the Dutch subcontractor and it was approved by us, by our customer, and by the regulatory agency. To start everything from scratch after three months into the project was not acceptable.

Another option was to find the special steel at a distributor at a premium price and airfreight it to California for manufacturing and testing per the Dutch contractor's design drawings. This option was also dropped since it was going to strain our manufacturing department and this new load on our manufacturing would delay other projects.

Another option was to go to the German steel mill with our subcontractor and negotiate for overtime work and extra funding for faster delivery. This option was also dropped since our special steel order was a small dent in their total steel production scheme. Our subcontractor had dealt with them face to face many times and the German steel producer would not budge.

A good option that everyone agreed upon was to search the world for this special steel during the next week to see if we could find it at a premium price. The steel had to be manufactured in a customer-qualified country. The steel had to have material test certificates for the regulatory agency. We agreed that we would share the premium price for the purchase of this special steel with our subcontractor and also share airfreight costs to the Netherlands with them. My company assigned me three full-time purchasing agents to search for this material all over the world.

After the emergency meeting, I called my customer in Norway and explained the unfortunate delays in the special steel delivery. I outlined the steps that we are taking along with our subcontractor to remedy the issue. Our customer was very upbeat with our proactive steps. The project manager at my customer informed me first verbally and then in writing that they would accept a month delay in the delivery of the completed systems in Malaysia without applying any liquidated damages to my company. This was great news for my company.

It took us three days to find the special steel with all the required test certificates at a secondhand supplier in Houston, Texas, at a premium price. We split the extra cost of the material with our subcontractor and we airfreighted 30 tons of material to the Netherlands. My quality engineer on-site, the Dutch subcontractor, and I worked on a modified fabrication, test, and acceptance schedule for the hydraulic cylinders. The Dutch subcontractor worked very diligently and overtime, when necessary, with my quality engineer watching over every step of the way. They completed the hydraulic cylinders one month late per the new schedule and airfreighted them to California for final assembly and testing. We were exactly a month late in the project when the completed systems were ready for customer acceptance. When my customer came to our facilities to accept the final systems, they informed us that the overall project had been delayed so we did not have to airfreight the completed assemblies to Malaysia. I wished I knew about this project delay a little earlier. However, we completed the systems one month late and they were accepted by our customer without a hitch. Acceptance sign off was a big milestone payday for my company.

As the project manager, I learned a lot from this special steel sourcing fiasco by our subcontractor. Even if my subcontractor was a very dependable one, I should have implanted my own engineer at their site and gotten daily updates on this critical item. I should have asked my subcontractor to line up a backup source for the special steel if the German one failed to deliver. Also, I should have required our purchasing department to include late penalty clauses for critical milestones such as the special steel delivery date to our subcontractor's contract.

On the positive side, the issue was solved by working very closely with the subcontractor. I helped them all I could to remedy the issue. My company was generous enough to share the extra costs for the material and shipping. One thing I did not allow was for my company to squeeze the subcontractor into a corner and beat him up to get the job done. Subcontractors are crucial parts of the project team. Working together and helping them in all aspects of their portion of the project is a must for a healthy project conclusion.

LESSONS LEARNED FROM THIS PROJECT EVENT

- Follow your subcontractor's progress very closely.
- Always implant your people at your crucial subcontractors to monitor on-site progress of your project.
- If your purchased items are a small fish in a big pond, persistently make sure that your items are not pushed aside.
- Always consider several feasible options in order to get out of a bind in a project.

Case 4.2: Union Strike in France

I was managing a project to build an oil platform mooring system for a new rig in the Gulf of Mexico. There were several design engineers, subcontractors, and consultants on my team. One of the subcontractors was in France. They were assigned to build high-pressure hydraulic cylinders per our specifications. The project started on time and the first couple of months went without any incidents. In the beginning of the third month, I received a telephone call from my subcontractor's project manager in France. He told me that his machinists might go on strike in the next couple of weeks. There was a slowdown in their work pace during contract negotiations. He assured me that his management was negotiating with the machinists union and they would settle their differences before their contract deadline.

I started to get worried. I informed my upper management about the potential strike in France. We had no choice but to wait for the results of their negotiations. A couple of days passed and I received no update from my counterpart at the French subcontractor. Finally, I called him and explained my concerns about delaying the hydraulic cylinders for my project. He again assured me that they were at the final details of the contract negotiations. He was going to let me know the results in 24 hours. The next day came and I anxiously waited for his phone call. The telephone finally rang at 9 a.m. and my counterpart at the French subcontractor informed me with regret that the machinists voted to strike and they did not accept the company's terms for the new contract. He again assured me that this would be a short-term strike and work slowdown and the strike would not affect the delivery of my hydraulic cylinders.

I immediately had an emergency meeting with my upper management and our purchasing department director. During the meeting, I proposed a couple of options to get out of the French strike dilemma. Before the meeting I discussed the level of completion of our hydraulic cylinders with my subcontractor's project manager. All components, assemblies, and machining were about 40% complete when the strike started. One option was to ship everything to our plant in the United States and to complete them there. Our president assured me that we would not have the capacity to complete the job on time. Then we decided to look for other high-pressure hydraulic cylinder builders around the world that had enough capacity to complete our job in a timely fashion. I was going to lose another week or two while negotiating and signing a contract with a new subcontractor. Also, partially completed cylinder shipments from France to our new subcontractor would have taken at least a week with an expedited shipment. We gave our purchasing director top priority to find a new subcontractor to complete the hydraulic cylinders for my project.

The purchasing director started to contact all the other hydraulic cylinder manufacturers that we had dealt with in the past. Luckily, he found one in the Netherlands that had enough capacity to complete our job on time. They negotiated the terms of the contract by teleconferencing and signed the contract online. I informed my customer's project manager of what was going on with the hydraulic cylinders project. He agreed with my approach and he even suggested several hydraulic manufacturers to our purchasing director. We called our subcontractor in France too and told them what we were trying to do. They agreed with us too, since they could not propose any other viable option to us. We paid 40% of our contract to our subcontractor in France. They agreed to truck the partially completed hydraulic cylinders to our new Dutch subcontractor on their own nickel.

Two trucks had to be loaded at the French subcontractor's plant at night in order not to interfere with the strikers during the day. With a two-week delay, the partially completed hydraulic cylinders arrived at our new Dutch subcontractor's facilities. The Dutch subcontractor completed, tested, and shipped the hydraulic cylinders to us on time. The French subcontractor's strike lasted 10 weeks. If I had stayed with the French subcontractor, my project's entire schedule would have been destroyed. I would have had a very dissatisfied and angry customer even if the contract with our customer covered us as harmless for unforeseen strike events.

These kinds of unforeseen events can occur on any project. As the project manager, it is my responsibility to find other routes to bypass these blockades. Extra efforts made to move the project along smoothly make my customer and my upper management very happy and raise their confidence in me.

LESSONS LEARNED FROM THIS PROJECT EVENT

- Labor unions are very strong and labor strikes are very common in some countries.
- Changing subcontractors in the middle of a project can be very risky and requires very detailed and accurate planning.
- Sometimes, as project managers, we have to make bold moves in order to get our projects going in the right direction.

Case 4.3: A Scheduling Challenge

I was assigned to manage a data communication chip design and test project with a team of 16 engineers and two international subcontractors. The project duration was a year. Initially, I put together a project schedule in a week that included all domestic and international resources, all dependencies between tasks, all critical document delivery dates to the customer, all internal and customer design review meetings, the customer's acceptance test dates, and payment milestones. I also included all the pertinent holidays and forecasted special events for each team member. The whole project schedule ended up being a 570-line monster file on MS Project. I did not have anyone helping me on scheduling. The schedule was a very dynamic document. I had to update it daily and I had to present it to my team, to my upper management, and to my customer on a weekly basis. The schedule updates, estimating work-performed percentages, and finding errors in the schedule took a tremendous amount of my time. I was falling behind in managing my team's people and my subcontractors.

Work scheduled and work performed were critical inputs to my earned value analysis for my project. I had to be fairly accurate in my work-performed estimates. These work-performed estimates went directly into my project's schedule performance indices and cost performance indices. My management judged my project's progress and health with these indices.

I had to do my scheduling in a more efficient and a more accurate way. I decided to break down the monster schedule file into 12 major task groups and two subcontractor groups. Each major task group's schedule had about 40 tasks. Then I created a master schedule that included the results of major task groups, all critical document delivery dates to the customer, all internal and customer design review meetings, the customer's acceptance test dates, and payment milestones. I only presented the master schedule to my team, to my upper management, and to my customer. If they had questions about the progress being made in a major task group or at the subcontractor, I also presented that particular schedule to them.

This breakdown of the total schedule helped me a lot in managing the updates to schedules and reduced my time to almost half in dealing with my scheduling responsibilities. It was much easier to update smaller schedules and to find errors in them. During the review meetings, my team, my upper management, and my customer appreciated dealing with the master schedule. Schedule review times in the meetings got shorter. On average, we were spending an hour going over the monster schedule. With the master schedule, the schedule review times averaged about 20 minutes.

Creating the initial schedule took about a week. I had to discuss and finalize each task's duration, order, and dependencies with its owner. Each team member had to buy in to what he or she was committing to accomplish in a given time. Everyone on the team had a different work pace and work experience. It was crucial to understand the work performance rate of every one of my team members. I had to do the same thing with my two international subcontractors by teleconferencing. I included an 85% work production efficiency factor to the schedule. I had to include extensive training time for five of my novice team members. I tried to keep each task's duration between one and three weeks so that the task progress estimates could be predicted with accuracy. I included all the observed holidays for my domestic and international team members. For each team member, I included his or her personal time-off days during the project duration. Gathering all this data to input into MS Project was painstaking. It was worth the entire week I spent to gather all the pertinent data for scheduling.

For a large project like this data communication chip design and test project, I should have asked for a scheduler from my management to help me. Such a person was not in my project budget. He or she would have had to charge the company overhead or erode my project's margin. In hindsight, gathering all the scheduling data from my team members and from my international subcontractors gave me a good insight on everyone's capabilities and work performance rates.

LESSONS LEARNED FROM THIS PROJECT EVENT

- A well-prepared project schedule is a shining light on the health of your project.
- A large project schedule can be very cumbersome to update daily by a project manager.
- A large project schedule can be easily broken down into smaller ones and a master one.
- Work production efficiencies should also be included into necessary tasks with care.

Case 4.4: Task Management between Different Times Zones

I had a challenging project management responsibility for a global project that spanned five different time zones. The chip design project lasted for 18 months and covered the software design and verification phase, the chip prototype construction phase, and the volume production start-up phase. My customer was in Munich, Germany. I had four chip design engineers working for me in California. My engineers were assigned to design major segments of the chip and also test the functionality of the whole design. A segment of the chip was being designed by a subcontractor at the

Research Triangle, North Carolina. A second segment of the chip was being designed by an Indian design company in Bangalore. The prototypes of this high-performance chip were scheduled to be built at a specialty foundry in Tokyo, Japan. Volume production was destined for a semiconductor fabrication plant in Penang, Malaysia.

Time management in this global project environment was a very strenuous task for me. The project started in June during daylight savings time. My daily workday schedule was as follows:

Call customer in Munich: 7–8 a.m. California time and 4–5 p.m. Munich time.

Meetings with team members in California: 8 a.m. to 12 noon.

Call subcontractor at Research Triangle, North Carolina: 1–2 p.m. California time and 4–5 p.m. North Carolina time.

Time for other project tasks such as scheduling, earned value analysis, and so on: 2–4 p.m.

Call foundry in Tokyo: 4–5 p.m. California time and 8–9 a.m. the next day Tokyo time.

Call volume production plant in Penang: 5–6 p.m. California time and 8–9 a.m. the next day Penang time.

Call subcontractor in Bangalore from home: 9–10 p.m. California time and 9:30–10:30 a.m. the next day Bangalore time.

Before the phone calls, we e-mailed the topics we wanted to discuss during the call to each other, so that we could bring in the right participants for the phone call. I directed the phone calls with the agenda generated from the e-mails. I recorded the minutes of the phone calls and the action items with the responsible people and delivery dates. I released the minutes of every phone call through our document control and had them distributed to the appropriate people.

There was another issue hanging over my head. Some of the countries that I was dealing with did not use daylight savings time. Only the United States and the European Union (EU) used daylight savings time, but they started and ended daylight savings time on different dates. The United States started daylight savings time on the last Sunday in March, but the EU started it on the second Sunday in March. So during that two-week gap, I had to call my customer at 8–9 a.m., which corresponded to my customer's 4–5 p.m. The United States ended daylight savings time on the first Sunday in November, but the EU ended it on the last Sunday in October. So during that one-week gap, I had to call my customer at 6–7 a.m., which corresponded to my customer's 4–5 p.m.

When daylight savings time ended in the United States, my daily schedule was as follows:

> Call customer in Munich: 7–8 a.m. California time and 4–5 p.m. Munich time.
>
> Meetings with team members in California: 8 a.m. to 12 noon.
>
> Call subcontractor at Research Triangle, North Carolina: 1–2 p.m. California time and 4–5 p.m. North Carolina time.
>
> Time for other project tasks such as scheduling, earned value analysis, and so on: 2–3 p.m.
>
> Call foundry in Tokyo: 3–4 p.m. California time and 8–9 a.m. the next day Tokyo time.
>
> Call volume production plant in Penang: 4–5 p.m. California time and 8–9 a.m. the next day Penang time.
>
> Time for other project tasks: 5–6 p.m.
>
> Call subcontractor in Bangalore from home: 8–9 p.m. California time and 9:30–10:30 a.m. the next day Bangalore time.

Global projects such as this one put a lot of excessive strain on the project manager. There are numerous bumps on the way before you reach the finish line. Precise time management is the only way to smooth out and to monitor effectively the progress of your project. The object of my time scheduling was not to disturb the call schedules of my customers and my team members around the world. As a conscientious project manager, I took the daily call scheduling bumps on myself and I smoothed out everyone's call schedules related to my project.

LESSONS LEARNED FROM THIS PROJECT EVENT

- Time management for communications in a global engineering project has to be precise. Communication time rules have to be established at the beginning of your project.
- Engagement slots assigned to different global teams should not interfere with each other.
- Daylight savings time can cause confusion to and alter your communication schedules.

Case 4.5: Dealing with Critical Path Tasks

Critical path tasks on a global project can be very challenging for a project manager. Tasks that lie on the critical path of a project cannot be delayed without sacrificing the project's schedule performance and any delays in them most likely would ruin your project's cost performance. A global project manager has to doubly focus on critical path tasks. Several noncritical tasks can slip during execution of a project and can become critical.

In a rotary engine design and development project that I was heavily involved in, seals used between combustion chambers became a major issue. After our initial design and prototype build, structural integrity of the seals degraded fast. We had to perform a thorough failure analysis, redesign the seals, and retest them. At the beginning of the project, the seal design tasks had a handsome slack time for an iterative development process so that it was not on the project's critical path. After the third design iteration, seal design tasks moved up to the critical path. The project manager had to beef up the seal design team with several expert consultants and had daily meetings on it in order to achieve the final design. We finally achieved the life expectancy out of the seals after the fifth design iteration. It delayed the project by a month and had a 30% cost overrun for the seal design portion of the project. Sometimes at the beginning, a technologically leading-edge component's design looks simple and straightforward, but by the end it comes back to bite your project. When I look back on the seal design task history, other project approaches come to mind. If we had had the two expert consultants at the beginning of the task, we might have achieved our goal with a couple of design iterations within the allocated time and even within the allocated budget.

In another critical path task case, my project's chip software design team always got tangled with the customer's continual design modifications. The customer's change approval process was very bureaucratic and therefore it sometimes took a month to see the final approved change. Luckily, the project was managed on a time and material basis. So these delays did not hurt my company financially, but they affected the duration of several critical path tasks and the completion date of the project. Also, my team members' efficiency dropped substantially while waiting for approved design modifications. I discussed this issue several times with my customer's project manager. He insisted on waiting for the final approved design modifications before doing anything. I could not move my team members to other projects during these lull times. Our project's productivity dropped, but we still charged our time to the customer. A yearlong project lasted almost a year and a half.

In an electric bus design project, the batteries we purchased for the buses were leading state of the art critical items, but they were not on the critical path of the project. I had to call my battery supplier daily along with my purchasing agent in order to ensure that there were no issues in the manufacturing and delivery of my batteries.

More often than not, a critical path task can be assigned to a subteam in a faraway location in the United States or in another country. Managing such a critical path task can be very challenging. In such a case, I had to plant one of my engineers with a subteam in France for six months for the construction of several advanced hydraulic components for my project. On top of that, we had to teleconference twice a week to assure them that the critical task was moving along smoothly. We were able to tackle all the issues in a timely fashion and the critical task was completed successfully on time.

In another critical task case, during setting up and qualification of a new wafer factory, my senior sputtering equipment engineer jumped ship and moved to our competitor. I had to scramble to find a replacement, which was not easy at all. At the time, sputtering equipment engineers were on demand. Through our human resources department and my contacts, we did a very detailed search without finding any feasible replacement. I decided to groom one of my novice engineers for this critical task. I also decided to get help from the equipment supplier. We agreed that one of their seasoned engineers would come to our factory and qualify the new sputtering equipment and at the same time train my new engineer. This was an expensive option, but I had to go along with it in order to complete my project without any delay.

LESSONS LEARNED FROM THIS PROJECT EVENT

- During the execution of a global project, several non-critical tasks can easily slip back and become critical.
- Critical tasks have to be completed satisfactorily on time even if you experience cost overruns to finalize them.
- If you have a critical task that is being performed in a foreign country, you better have a constant and reliable observer at that location.

Case 4.6: Estimating Task Completion Percentages

As global project managers we have one of the most difficult and periodically required duties of estimating completion percentages for every task. Our project's schedule and cost performance indices depend on the accuracy of our estimates. We present these performance indices to our upper management and to our customer at least monthly. These performance indices also show us the health condition of our project. We can see the tasks that we are having issues with. In some tasks we are behind schedule and in a few others we are ahead of schedule. In some tasks we are over budget and in a few others we are under budget.

If possible, I always sat down monthly with the responsible task owner(s) and decided together on completion percentage(s) of his or her task(s). Task completion estimates became more blurred for task owners in other global locations and for our subcontractors. On many occasions, I had to travel to the site of the task owner in order to get more reliable task completion estimates. I have found throughout my project management career that most task owners overestimate their task completion percentage in order to present a rosy picture. If you peel back layers of his or her task and go into minute details then a more reliable task completion percentage picture emerges.

I had the most difficulty getting good task completion estimates from my software design engineers. The software design task was one issue, but testing the software and revising it and documenting it was another. For the most part, the software designer and the tester worked as a pair. When they told me that they were 90% complete, I could never believe them. The remaining 10% took forever to complete. I asked them to break down the software structure into manageable substructures or modules. We reviewed the status of each module. If I sensed any trouble in the progress of the software design process, I had to take immediate drastic action. Several times I had to call in experienced senior software design engineers to take over remaining tasks in order to complete the project on time even if I ran over budget.

Another area of difficult task completion percentage estimates was in design engineering calculations. I had separate task duration estimates in my project plan for design calculations and for checking these calculations. In most cases, the checker found several mistakes or missing items in the design calculations. Then calculations went back to the designer. The designer updated his calculations per the checker's recommendations and findings. Calculations went back to the checker again for rechecking. This iterative cycle sometimes lasted four or five times, especially in complicated and detailed calculations with new in-house generated software. I always ran behind schedule and over budget in extensive design engineering calculations.

Task completion percentages were also significantly affected by our customer's review of the design drawings. Most of the time, the customer was delayed in his or her review and approval of drawings. When we received the delayed review and comments back, there were always some minor tweaks to the design drawings, which did not change the scope of the project specifications. My designers had to update drawings and resubmit them for approval. This cycle was out of my control. I could not push my customers with the same intensity as I pushed my team members to get something done. Task completion estimates always tanked when a customer's action was involved.

Subcontractors always posed a problem in task completion estimates. If a subcontractor was falling behind schedule, I did not hear about it in a timely fashion so that we could formulate corrective actions together without any delay. More often than not, I had to implant engineers or purchasing agents into my subcontractor's facility in order to be able to follow with ease of mind what was going on with my project's tasks.

Most unreliable task completion estimates came from my global subteams. According to my subteam leader, especially in developing countries, everything was going "hunky-dory." When I visited them or sent one of my U.S.-based engineers to check on them, I always received different perceptions about task completions. My subteams in developing countries needed continual monitoring and hand-holding in order for me to be assured that their tasks were on time and within budget.

LESSONS LEARNED FROM THIS PROJECT EVENT

- Watch out for overestimated task completion estimates by your team members.
- You can run into surprising misunderstandings with task completion estimates for tasks being performed in foreign countries.
- Software design engineers and mechanical product design engineers tend to always overestimate their task completions.
- You have to watch your customers and your subcontractors like a hawk when it is time for task completion estimates.

5

CASE STUDIES IN RESOURCE MANAGEMENT

Resource management in a global environment gets very tricky and requires continual monitoring. In particular, a global project's budget management can be a constant struggle. Listening to experts and evaluating input from experienced people outside of your project team always helps to avoid pitfalls during the execution of your global project.

I had a challenging experience with my company's information technology department in one of my long-term projects. Computer and information technology was advancing at a mind-boggling speed at the turn of the century. A computer's operating system, processor, memory, and hard drive capacity became obsolete in six months. I took it upon myself to improve our information technology department in order to save my project in Case 5.1.

After two months into a high volume production project, our subcontractor in Japan announced that they were shutting down their operations which produced a critical component for our assembly in three months. This was quite a shock to me and to my company. Case 5.2 describes the actions that I took to remedy this issue.

While working with leading-edge technology small-sized subcontractors during a project, lots of unforeseen issues can pop up. Thoroughly understanding the capabilities of the personnel, equipment, and processes being used in these companies can cut down on undesirable issues as shown in Case 5.3.

In dealing with international project teams from different countries, there is always a difference in adrenaline rush and excitement for meetings and project tasks. I experienced an adrenaline rush and excitement toward project meetings and tasks at the higher end of the spectrum from team members in countries such as Japan and Germany and at the lower end of the spectrum from team members in countries

119

such as Malaysia, Mexico, and countries in the Mediterranean region. I detail my encounters in different countries in Case 5.4.

During the execution of a project, always keep the pressure on your team members, but do not overdo it and burn them out. In this day and age, continuous connectivity to our team members can be very hazardous and stressful, if it is not handled with care. Such events are detailed in Case 5.5.

Listening is the greatest virtue of a project manager. When I ran into trouble while executing a task, I listened to all ideas that would cure the issue at hand. Such a nagging problem is detailed in Case 5.6. After trying a new interface system for over a month in our wafer fabrication lines, we saw significant increases in wafer yields. Also, wafer throughputs improved. Holdups for a shutdown process decreased significantly. I made this new process engineering shift interface meeting a standard for our wafer factory.

If a task in a project reaches a fire-fighting mode, your decision-making process to cure the issue accelerates very fast. You are in an urgent rescue mode. After being in a fire-fighting mode for two weeks to troubleshoot a control panel via telephone conversations in a remote location in Norway with a novice engineer, I had to take drastic action as detailed in Case 5.7.

In some cases, we have to rescue our subcontractors from a bind. I tasked two engineers on my team to improve a critical Japanese supplier's falling yields. As a project manager, it was my responsibility to help my subcontractor in any way that I could. As a result of this urgent six-week long rescue mission, our product's final test yields improved immensely and they were steady. These details are given in Case 5.8.

Listening to all of the input regarding your project's tasks and filtering them down to useful ones is an art in itself. Such input is detailed in Case 5.9.

Some tasks in our global projects require us to deal with foreign government agencies. Bureaucracy in a foreign government can hurt your project in many ways. You have to go along with experts to solve your problems with bureaucrats even if it costs your project an arm and a leg as detailed in Case 5.10.

As global project managers, we have to be on top of all ancillary tasks such as shipping rules and regulations of our finished products. If we leave these ancillary tasks alone, they might harm our project tremendously in one way or another. In Case 5.11, I missed details of the insurance coverage for my project's finished products shipment.

At the bidding phase of a project, we might have to partner with other companies in order to strengthen our position. At the beginning of a project, all project partners look eager and willing to win the bid. Many unforeseen issues might surface with our project partners during the execution phase of the project. As project managers, it is our responsibility to remedy these project partner issues as fast as we can without damaging the cost and schedule performance of our project. An example is given in Case 5.12.

Sometimes cost performance of a task might be hit by unexpected increases in material costs. I had a project to design, build, and test 20 high-load capacity and high-pressure hydraulic cylinders for a customer in Brazil. I had to scramble to get my cost performance under control as detailed in Case 5.13.

Monitoring schedule and cost performance of a global project very closely at regular intervals is a must for a project manager. You have to bring your company's other departments in sync with your project's dynamic environment. The challenge is to be able to collect all schedule and cost performance data in a timely fashion from your foreign project partners as shown in Case 5.14.

Case 5.1: Dependence on Other Departments

During the execution of a project, a project manager depends on performances of other departments in the company. The purchasing department is the key player in purchased components for the project and in establishing contracts for subcontractors and consultants joining the project team. The accounting department has to execute correctly and in a timely fashion the project's payables and receivables and charges to project charge numbers. The drafting department has to prepare and release drawings, manufacturing process instructions, and quality assurance instructions according to promised schedules. The sales department has to coordinate with the project manager closely for a project's contract extension and for related competitive bids to a project. Every department in your company contributes to your project in one way or another during the execution phase.

I had a challenging experience with my company's information technology (IT) department in one of my long-term projects.

Computer and information technology were advancing at a mind-boggling speed at the turn of the century. A computer's operating system, processor, memory, and hard drive capacity became obsolete in six months. You had to improve your computer's performance at most in a year in order to keep up with the changing world. In parallel to improved computer performance, software that was used in my projects was going through revisions to utilize enhances in hardware performance. I had an IT department in my company, as the saying goes, that always liked to squeeze the lemon to the last drop. They dragged their feet in upgrading my team's hardware, software, and communication tools. This type of mentality affected the performance of my engineers who always wanted to be in sync with leading-edge technology. When I made an upgrade request, it took them two to four weeks to respond. I had several meetings with the head of our IT department regarding timely upgrades to our IT tools. I told him how demoralizing the situation was for my engineers. I told him that if our IT tools were not at the leading edge of technology then our company could not stay at the leading edge for long. He kept complaining about his budgetary and personnel issues. He did not change his style of service a bit to my requests. After two months of frustration, I went up the ladder to his boss. I called a meeting with the IT manager and his boss. I went over all hardware, software, and communication, especially videoconferencing, issues. I sensed during the meeting that the IT manager was being protected by his boss. Changes were not going to happen as swiftly as I liked. Their vision was to reduce the IT department's budget and use all IT tools that we had as long as possible.

Then I went and discussed the IT department issues with other department heads. All department heads had similar complaints to mine, but their complaints were not as urgent as mine. I convinced all department heads that something had to be done fast to change the existing IT department mission. Two of the other department heads and myself agreed to take our case a notch higher to the president of the company. I called a meeting with our president and also invited the IT department manager's boss to the meeting.

The meeting with the president, the IT department manager's boss, two department heads, and I lasted over two hours. I presented all my team's IT department issues that I encountered during the execution of my project. The other two department heads presented their issues too. The IT department manager's boss was continually in a protective mood. At the end of the meeting, our president promised to take constructive action immediately to improve the situation. A week passed and I got the news that our IT department head had resigned or been let go. There was also reshuffling of responsibilities in upper management. The IT department started to report directly to the president. The company searched and hired a new vice president of IT from a well-known computer technology company. After six months of continual struggle, my engineers and I started to see a bright light at the end of the IT tunnel.

The execution of a project can be bogged down and sometimes a project manager can experience long delays and cost overruns to his project's tasks due to poor performance by other departments in a company. Taking immediate action to correct issues at hand with other departments is a must. The whole company has to run smoothly and efficiently on all cylinders in order to complete a project successfully.

LESSONS LEARNED FROM THIS PROJECT EVENT

- The IT department is a very crucial segment of your company in this day and age.
- Getting consensus with department heads to solve an issue gathers momentum and helps you to achieve your goal in a timely fashion.
- All departments in your company have to function well in order for your project to succeed.

Case 5.2: Subcontractor Announcement of Shutting Down Operations

We were qualified and were running a high volume production of computer subassemblies for a U.S. computer manufacturer. A critical component for our computer subassemblies was being supplied by a sole source Japanese subcontractor. After two months into the high volume production, our subcontractor in Japan announced that they were shutting down their operations that produced the critical component in three months. This was quite a shock to me and to my company. At that time, I was heading the engineering team for volume production of computer subassemblies. I immediately had several telephone conversations with our subcontractor to understand the reasoning behind their unexpected shutdown. Apparently, the critical component manufacturing was not profitable enough for them and the new president of the company decided to end this division's operations. My company proposed several options to keep them going until high volume production of computer subassemblies for our U.S. computer manufacturer continued. To qualify a new subcontractor for this critical component would be a tremendous undertaking at this stage of the game. My company offered to help them financially or even buy their division out to no avail.

I told our president that we should not inform our U.S. customer until we had a detailed solid plan to qualify alternate sources for this critical component. Our president agreed with me and assigned me to prepare the qualification plan in three working days. After the internal review of the qualification plan, we were going to go to our customer and present it in person.

I had three alternate subcontractor choices for this critical component. One was in the Bay Area. The second one was again in Japan, and the third one was in Malaysia. I immediately went to our purchasing director and asked him to find out in two days their available production capacities for this critical component and their pricing. These were the two most important inputs to start our qualification plan. It turned out that the sum of any two of the subcontractors' production capacities could satisfy our needs. We ranked these three subcontractors with the purchasing manager using several critical criteria such as quality control, product reliability, stability of the subcontractor, pricing, and capacity. The subcontractors in the Bay Area and in Japan came in on top. We decided to prepare qualification plans with these two subcontractors and present them to our customer.

I called our customer's project manager immediately and explained the unfortunate upcoming snag to our volume production. I detailed our course of action with two new subcontractors. I also detailed the qualification plans that we would be pursuing in the next three months. I emphasized their involvement in the qualification process. Our customer had to evaluate 200 computer subassemblies, 100 from each new subcontractor, with new critical components in two weeks. Our customer's project manager agreed to do his part on time so that we would not disrupt the volume production process.

I sent two engineering teams, one to each potential subcontractor, for a detailed qualification process. Major areas of concern were operator training, product change control, quality control, and incoming material control. It took the teams one week to evaluate these two potential subcontractors. Both teams had very promising reports about these two new subcontractors. We decided to bring both subcontractors on board on equal footing. We did not want to rely heavily on one of them. Both subcontractors provided us with qualification components with measured critical parameters in four weeks. Then we built computer subassemblies for qualification using these new critical components in five weeks.

I hand carried the qualification lots to our customer. They tested 200 computer subassemblies in their computers while I watched over their shoulders. Fortunately, there were no surprises. Our customer's project manager gave us the green light to use the new critical component in our computer subassemblies as promised in two weeks.

This surprising change to our product came without adequate warning. I had to adapt to this change fast. I had to also convince my customer about the steps I was taking to deal with this change. We were lucky that there were other alternate solutions to this problem. My mistake was originally to go with a single source for the critical component. I should have qualified at least two subcontractors for this critical component at the beginning of the volume production process.

LESSONS LEARNED FROM THIS PROJECT EVENT

- A surprising event can occur unexpectedly at a reliable subcontractor.
- Prepare a detailed and complete alternate plan before approaching your customer with a way out of the showstopper.
- Always qualify multiple sources for critical components of your project.

Case 5.3: Subcontracting to Small Leading-Edge Technology Companies

Subcontracting to small leading-edge technology companies can be very tricky and time consuming during the execution of a global project. Continual monitoring of such companies is a must in order to assure that they are always up to a high level of operational standards and their personnel turnover does not hamper your project's progress.

I was leading a team of engineers to supply high-volume magnetic recording sensors to our customers around the globe. Our supply chain originated in our wafer fabrications in California and branched into higher assemblies in South Korea, Malaysia, Singapore, and Puerto Rico. Surfaces of our read-write sensors had to be free of any contaminants before being installed into disk drives. Our final operations were performed in class-10 clean room environments. We were supplying thousands of sensors a week to different customers. Our major sensor lot rejection cause by customers was contamination. Several lots per week were put on hold or rejected by our customers for sensor surface contamination. I had a subteam whose mission was to identify surface contaminants, track down their sources, and eliminate them from occurring again.

For U.S. customers, we brought contaminated sensors to our material evaluation laboratories in California. We did failure analysis using advanced state of the art auger spectroscopy, energy dispersive x-ray spectroscopy, and atomic force microscopy. We had well-trained technicians in all three shifts. We were able to get surface analysis reports in a day to respond with our corrective actions to our customers. Fast turnaround in corrective action was a must in just-in-time supplier chain requirements from our customers. I had to set up failure analysis laboratories for our customer centers in Singapore, Japan, and Europe.

My team and I searched and sourced three leading-edge technology contamination evaluation laboratories in each location. I sent my engineers to these laboratories for qualification. We explained our failure analysis requirements for surface contaminants on our sensors. We checked their operations, financial stability, measurement costs, type of equipment they had for measurements, equipment downtime, equipment repair structure, equipment spare parts situation, their technicians' measurement training and experience, sample preparation techniques, measurement prioritization and turnaround time, failure analysis reporting time table, and so on. After a thorough comparative analysis, we chose one laboratory at each location to be our failure analysis center.

My team and I had to check on these three leading-edge technology laboratories periodically. We had to make sure that they were upgrading their equipment to the most advanced ones that provided accurate elemental and chemical compositions of contaminants on the surfaces of our sensors. We had to make sure that they were not losing their experienced technicians. We had some issues with lost sensors and miscommunication. We were constantly discussing how to improve and how to expedite our failure analyses within our partnership.

Several times while the failure analysis was going on, I had to send one of my engineers and a couple of inspectors to my customer's facilities to sort our sensors. We had to separate good sensors from contaminated ones under high-powered microscopes in a Class-10 clean room environment so that my customer's automated assembly lines would not slow down or come to a halt due to the lack of our sensors.

In a just-in-time high-volume relationship with our customers, I had to form such a global failure analysis group with leading-edge technology small laboratories. It took my team and me six months to form our failure analysis network, but in the end it worked out very successfully for many years to come. Our customers were very satisfied with our response time and corrective actions to contamination issues in our magnetic recording sensors.

LESSONS LEARNED FROM THIS PROJECT EVENT

- To qualify small leading-edge technology companies for your project will require extensive scrutinizing and will take more time.
- To set up a global network for a crucial project task is always a challenge for a project manager.

Case 5.4: Latitude versus Attitude

When dealing with international project teams from different countries, there was always a difference in adrenaline rush and excitement toward meetings and project tasks. I experienced adrenaline rush and excitement toward project meetings and tasks at the higher end of the spectrum from team members in countries such as Japan and Germany and at the lower end of the spectrum from team members in countries such as Malaysia, Mexico, and countries in the Mediterranean region.

I dealt with team members from Malaysia, Mexico, and Southern Turkey who often claimed that they never committed to completing a given task on a mutually determined completion time. Their behavior was inconsistent and uncooperative, and they ignored my multiple requests and task deadlines. They had to be micromanaged and pushed to complete a task with quality. They had a lackadaisical work behavior. Of course this behavior was not true for all team members from those regions, but most of them had lower concentration and negative behavior. I attributed this kind of behavior to the warm and humid climate in those countries and to their traditional work ethics.

In colder climates such as in Japan and Germany, people developed survival intelligence, they became practical, aggressive, and competitive. Science and technology mushroomed from these kinds of behaviors in the Western world.

For example, during my projects in Malaysia, I had issues with my team members coming to meetings late and not being prepared. Some team members walked into the conference room 10 or 15 minutes late. Some of them did not have a clue as to what they had to present or what to contribute at that meeting. They obviously did not read their meeting invitation e-mail in detail. I constantly reminded my team members that meetings were not for kicking back and for being in another world. Everyone had to be on their toes and contribute during a meeting even if it was not their turn to present their part. I joked with the latecomers to the meetings that I was going to charge a U.S. dollar per minute that they were late to the meeting so that we could all go out and have a feisty lunch every week. I kindly asked the latecomers to be on time to the meetings with no success. Then I went to their supervisors and asked them kindly to correct the situation by talking to their people. The supervisors' discussions with their people helped the situation a little, but it was difficult to get rid of bad habits. Then I went up to the general manager of the company and asked him to issue a stern memorandum for timely attendance and well preparedness to all meetings. The stern memorandum did the trick and all my team members got the message. After two months of determination, my team meetings got into a productive and a precise rhythm.

I also had issues with promised action item completion times in countries such as Malaysia, Mexico, and countries in the Mediterranean region. If I were given an action item completion time by a Japanese engineer, the task was done before or right at the promised completion time. If a Japanese engineer had problems with completing his task, he came and asked me for help or for an extension to complete the promised action item. However, in Mexico if an engineer promised me an action item completion time, he came with his results a day to a week late. In these warm regions of the world, the only way to keep my team members on their toes was to micromanage them. I had to talk to them daily or even hourly to push them and to monitor their progress in a given task.

Most of my team members in these warmer regions of the world also had a relaxed behavior toward our customers and our subcontractors. I emphasized that when a customer or a subcontractor visited our plant we had to be well prepared and had to be sharp.

I want to emphasize that these lackadaisical behaviors surfaced in the majority of my team members and not in all of them. It is very difficult to change human behaviors in other countries. You have to be flexible, adjust, and learn how to deal with the situation at hand. Jimmy Buffett's song lyrics describe project team members' behavior in different countries well. "With these changes in latitudes, changes in attitudes, nothing remains quite the same."

LESSONS LEARNED FROM THIS PROJECT EVENT

- In a global project environment, work habits and attitudes vary vastly from country to country.
- Changing well-ingrained habits in your global team members can take lots of patience and continual guidance on your part to correct.

Case 5.5: Stress from 24/7 Connectivity

Internet and cell phone connections are getting faster, cheaper, and more reliable every day. These wireless connections are achieved from anywhere on Earth, even flying at 35,000 feet above the ground or while vacationing on a remote Tahitian island. Continual advances in e-mailing, tweeting, cell phoning, text messaging, ease of data transfer, videoconferencing, and wireless networking make the life of a global project manager much easier. Anyone on your project team can instantly work with their files, programs, and networks from anywhere on Earth just as if they were at their own desks. A global project manager has to lay down ground rules for 24/7 communication with all team members, including subcontractors and customers around the world, at kickoff meetings of a project.

During the execution phase of a global project, a team member can get inundated by e-mails, cell phone calls, text messages, and so forth. These 24/7 communications can occur during lunchtime, dinner time, sleep time, or even during weekends, holidays, and vacations. A conscientious team member will try to respond to all messages in a timely fashion while sacrificing his or her personal life. These kinds of 24/7 connections can cause overload and burn out team members and the project manager fast. A 24/7-connected environment will bring good things to a global project, but the global project manager has to orchestrate and apply a fair balance between continuous connectivity and the private life of every team member so that stress levels stay at normal levels during the execution of a global project.

A good engineering friend of mine was working on an international company's restructuring project team. He was a very conscientious worker. He checked his e-mails every half an hour from the time he woke up until he went to bed. He always answered his cell phone. One Saturday night we agreed to go out to dinner together. He made a reservation at a good Italian restaurant, which was very hard to get into. He brought his girlfriend. I brought my wife. We were about to sit at our reserved table and his cell phone rang. He answered his phone and ran out of the restaurant to talk to the caller. We sat down at our table and waited for my friend to return. After five minutes he returned with a very sullen face. He told us that the call came from his project manager. His project manager urgently wanted a couple of graphs from him during the next hour. My friend told his project manager that he was at dinner with us, but his project manager insisted on his untimely demand. My friend had to excuse himself from dinner and go home to his laptop. I learned later that his project manager was a workaholic and was very rigid with his untimely demands. He sometimes called my friend at midnight and during weekends with excessive requests. My friend worked on that project team for a month and then gave his notice to leave the company. He was totally stressed out from 24/7 connectivity to his team and from an unreasonably demanding project manager. My friend immediately started his own company and became quite successful. In a way he was thankful for his previous project manager's unacceptable behavior.

Interactive design and development by teams around the globe are also an integral part of a global project. I was the project manager of a chip design team in California that was constantly interfacing with our German counterparts. Eight hours of time difference between the two design locations made me structure feasible meeting and interaction times in order to reduce work stress on both parties. I even allowed two of my design engineers to work the night shift in California for two months in order to have real-time interaction with their German counterparts. The proposal to work the night shift in real time with the Germans during the design of the chip's software was suggested by my engineers. Real-time interaction between two design parties reduced time and error in completing their design tasks.

A project manager colleague of mine was working with a sub-team in India to manufacture computer components. A twelve and a half hour time difference between India and California required him to take several steps to reduce work-related stress from continuous connectivity. He set up videoconferencing from 7:30 p.m. to 9 p.m. California time on every Monday. He asked his California team members not to call their Indian teammates from 6:30 a.m. to 7:30 p.m. California time during the work week and during weekends. He also listed all Indian holidays when communication was to be stopped. The project manager had to establish these communication rules for his project during the kickoff phase of his project.

LESSONS LEARNED FROM THIS PROJECT EVENT

- Stress levels of your global team members can increase exponentially in a 24/7-connected environment.
- 24/7-communication rules between your global team members, your global customers, and your global sub-contractors have to be laid out by you at the kickoff meetings of a project.

Case 5.6: Engineering Interface among Wafer Fabrication Shifts

Wafer fabrication engineering requires detailed recording and correcting for out-of-specification conditions, scrap reasons, equipment malfunctions, corrective actions, and variations in control charts. Our wafer factory was working in three shifts for seven days. Wafer fabrications process engineering hours were 7 a.m. to 3 p.m. for the day shift, 3 p.m. to 11 p.m. for the swing shift, and 11 p.m. to 7 a.m. for the night shift. I had six process engineers in each shift. One was a principal process engineer for deposition processes and the backup for ion milling processes. The second one was a principal engineer for ion milling processes and the backup for deposition processes. The third one was a principal process engineer for photolithography and the backup for plate and etching processes. The fourth process engineer was the principal for plate and etch processes and the backup for photolithography. The fifth process engineer was the principal for wafer testing and the backup for clean room environment. My sixth process engineer was the principal for the clean room environment and the backup for wafer testing. All the important events that happened during a shift were recorded in six different logbooks, one for every process center, and critical action items were being sent to the next shift's engineers by using six different e-mail folders, again one for every process center.

The system was working okay, but it was not perfect. Several items, some of them critical, were falling through the cracks. There were misinterpretations of messages written in logbooks and in e-mail folders. I was getting several telephone calls a night from the swing shift and the night shift engineers asking me to explain some of the comments written about a process or about malfunctioning equipment. Even I could not help explain some of the condensed phrases. Comments like "sputtering equipment 1 is acting" and "photolithography curing plates had temperature problems" were causing us to do extensive detective work to find the particular malfunction. We had to improve our wafer yields continually and the process engineering communication system between shifts was hampering our progress. I had several meetings with my engineers from every shift and we discussed in detail how to improve our communication procedures between shifts. We decided to record more precise and detailed information regarding every issue during a shift. All of my engineers complied very well, but still it was not a good communication system between the shifts.

We had over 200 operations and equipment in six process centers in the wafer factory. This kind of very dynamic and continuous process environment did not allow any mistakes or any shortcuts to overcome the issues that popped up. All of the sputtering engineers had to be on the same page on all shifts. All of the photolithography engineers had to be on the same page, even on the same line, on all shifts.

During one of my process engineering meetings, one of the engineers proposed a good idea to extend our shift hours by half an hour and have a face to face between the shift engineers. I talked to every engineer and got their consent to extend their work hour by half an hour. I also talked with human resources to make sure that we were not violating any overtime regulations. Salaried engineers did not get paid for overtime in this company. Everyone agreed to the new schedule and to the shift interaction meeting.

Wafer fabrications process engineering new hours were 7 a.m. to 3:30 p.m. for the day shift, 3 p.m. to 11:30 p.m. for the swing shift, and 11 p.m. to 7:30 a.m. for the night shift. We started to have process engineering shift interface meetings from 7 a.m. to 7:30 a.m. for the night shift and day shift engineers, from 3 p.m. to 3:30 p.m. for the day shift and swing shift engineers, and from 11 p.m. to 11:30 p.m. for the swing shift and night shift engineers. I attended all three meetings every day. I took the meeting notes and distributed action items list to the appropriate people. Sometimes we could not complete all current issues in a half an hour meeting. Some meetings extended to an hour.

After trying this new interface system for over a month, we saw significant increases in wafer yields. Also, wafer throughputs improved. Holdups for a shutdown process decreased significantly. I made this new process engineering shift interface meeting a standard for our wafer factory. I also covered the extra time that engineers were spending in these shift interface meetings in their annual bonus awards. My boss and the company president agreed to award extra bonuses for my process engineers for their voluntary agreement to spend extra time for shift interface meetings, which caused our wafer yields to improve continually.

LESSONS LEARNED FROM THIS PROJECT EVENT

- 24/7-production operations require face-to-face interaction between shift engineers and operators.
- Depending on only written communications between production shifts can cause misinterpretations.
- Written communication plus face-to-face interaction between production shifts reduces the possibility of errors.

Case 5.7: Fire Fighting during the Installation of a System on an Offshore Oil Platform

I was the project manager of a large project to design, build, and install an automated positioning system on a new offshore oil platform. The design and construction of the system were completed in the United States. The system components were shipped to Norway for installation. I had to send an application engineer to Norway to see the installation of the positioning system on the new oil platform and train the responsible people from our customer's team for its operation and maintenance.

I had a young and very inquisitive engineer on my team who was trained for six months during the construction and testing of the system in our facilities. He knew all the intricate details of the automated system. He was also well versed in troubleshooting the system components. I decided to send him to Norway for three months to oversee the installation of the system and to train the customer's team members. I discussed his mission with him. He was very excited and elated that he was going to represent our company by himself in such a detailed project. I told him that we were going to have a daily telephone conference five times a week. I promised him that I would bring in other design specialists to the telephone conference calls if there were any issues during the installation. I asked him to keep an engineering notebook to record all the daily tasks, mishaps, issues, and all important facts regarding the system installation. I also cautioned him to carry along a complete toolbox to be used during the system installation and some cold weather clothing.

The first month in Norway went well. The engineer did a great job during the installation of our automated positioning system. We had a telephone conference call at 8 a.m. California time and 5 p.m. Norway time during every working day. There were some minor issues such as interference with another equipment, which was solved by removing a quarter of an inch from the side flanges of our equipment. Several bolting patterns with the oil rig floor did not match. We had to slot our bolting holes to match theirs. Installation was completed in a month and test runs were starting. My engineer was freezing in Norway in the month of February, but he was upbeat and ready to start the test runs.

The control panel of the system started to have problems during the test runs. Watertight pressure switches were not sometimes switching at their set points. My engineer on location tried to find the cause of this intermittent malfunction without any success. I immediately collected the available brains in our plant and an application engineer from the pressure switch manufacturer and brainstormed the control panel problem in Norway. We provided several suggestions to our engineer over the telephone for him to try. Nothing seemed to work to correct this malfunction. We tried all the fire-fighting ideas for two weeks without any success.

I had another option. There was a very experienced consultant in electro-mechanical system design. My company used his services from time to time in the design of our control panels. I tried to reach him by telephone and by e-mail. I learned from his family that he was on a sailing vacation in Tahiti for a month. I asked his family as to how I could touch base with him. Apparently, he called his family at least twice a week when he was on land. I asked his family to help me to touch base with him on a crucial issue. I asked them to ask the consultant to call me as soon as possible.

After two days, I received a call from the consultant from Bora Bora in Tahiti. I explained the situation and told him that we were in a bind. I asked him if he could cut his vacation short and fly from Tahiti to Norway and help my resident engineer solve our control panel issue. I proposed an incentive to help him make up his mind. I told him that I would pay him his regular hourly rate even during his travel time and reimburse him for business class airline fares. He agreed to my proposal and promised me that he would be on the first flight out of Tahiti to Europe.

After troubleshooting the control panel together with my novice engineer in a very methodical way, the consultant found the problem that was causing our control panel to malfunction. The power that was feeding the control panel was sometimes below the allowable lower limit and was causing the pressure switches to not function properly.

Being in a fire-fighting mode for two weeks to troubleshoot the control panel by telephone conversations in a remote location in Norway with a novice engineer did not work out well. My hindsight told me that I should have sent my novice engineer to this important offshore assignment in a foreign country along with an experienced engineer as a team. In the end, my customer was not happy because it took us three weeks to troubleshoot the control panel malfunction. We were lucky that we were not penalized for this delay because the new oil platform had other functional issues. My solution to our problem was an expensive one. I was over budget and my management was not thrilled about it.

I thanked my consultant for saving our butt by cutting his vacation short. I showed my gratitude to him with a bonus payment. I did not forget to praise my novice engineer for performing a very detailed and a courageous job by himself working the first time on an oil platform. He also received an outstanding performance review from our customer's project manager.

LESSONS LEARNED FROM THIS PROJECT EVENT

- In a project, sometimes it takes very unusual and expensive decisions to solve a nagging problem.
- A novice engineer and an experienced engineer working as a team on a complicated project task can be more efficient and more effective.

Case 5.8: Engineers Sent to Japan to Improve Manufacturing Yields

A Japanese supplier was providing ceramic magnetic recording heads for our head stack assemblies for a U.S. disk drive manufacturer. Each head stack assembly was being tested for performance and the yields were low. We formed a team of six engineers, two from design, two from quality, and two from manufacturing, to improve the yields of our head stack assemblies. I was heading the yield improvement team. We investigated every process in our plant. We tracked every supplier's component lots to final testing. We realized that our final test yields were varying from 30% to 70% depending on the ceramic magnetic recording head lots we received from Japan. There were wide swings in performance of ceramic performance heads from lot to lot.

I called the chief engineer at our Japanese supplier and discussed our surprising conclusion for low product yields with him. He promised he would investigate his processes and report his findings to me in a week. A week passed and I did not hear anything from him. I called him again to emphasize the yield issue. He finally spilled the dire situation he was in. He told me that he was down to one manufacturing engineer. He lost two of them recently. He could not investigate and control all the processes for our ceramic magnetic recording heads. I proposed to help him by sending two of my seasoned manufacturing engineers from my team to Japan for four weeks. I asked his company to pay for travel expenses for my two engineers. He accepted my offer. Two of my team's senior manufacturing engineers, one a lapping expert and the other a grinding expert, were off to Japan.

We had a mission-defining meeting before the two engineers left. I wanted a daily update via e-mail from them detailing their investigation steps, their design-of-experiments, and their findings. We were also going to have a telephone conference call twice a week on Mondays and Thursdays at 5 p.m. Pacific standard time, namely, 9 a.m. on Tuesdays and Fridays in Japan.

My two engineers started to go over each manufacturing step of ceramic magnetic recording heads at our Japanese supplier. Some of the inconsistencies in their processes and in different shifts were corrected. These did not make any difference in our overall yields. I asked them to conduct several design-of-experiments involving lapping and grinding processes and especially speeds and send me products from these experiments by specifying all variables for a given lot. We built these special ceramic magnetic recording head lots to final assemblies and tested them to see the changes in final test yields.

The Japanese manufacturing personnel were helping my engineers day and night. They were doing up to 10 different experiments at once. We could not finish all the designed experiments in four weeks. We had to extend their stay in Japan another four weeks. At the end of the sixth week, we received several special lots with slower lapping and grinding speeds. Our final test yields with these slower speed lots shot up to 90%. The stresses induced on the ceramic slider body were much lower and therefore the stresses induced on the magnetic sensor were much reduced. I gave my engineers and the Japanese chief engineer the exciting good news. I asked them to send me five more confirmation lots with slower lapping and grinding speeds. All these special lots too went through final testing with flying colors. We had a very steady 90% final test yield.

Apparently, the Japanese manufacturing engineers increased lapping and grinding speeds to jack up the throughput due to increased demand from us. I emphasized to the Japanese chief engineer not to change anything in their processes without my approval. He agreed to it. He was very apologetic about the whole chaos that was created by his novice engineers.

After all the 24/7 work that my manufacturing engineers performed in Japan, I asked them to relax and spend a couple of days at their leisure before heading back. The Japanese chief engineer took them to a close by ash-spewing volcano and to some hot springs (*onsen*) near the volcano. My team's two manufacturing engineers did a great job performing a very structured design-of-experiments at our ceramic magnetic recording head supplier. I wrote a praising review regarding their excellent work in Japan to their supervisor and sent a copy of my review to our human resources.

This Japanese supplier was a critical part of our product. As a project manager, it was my responsibility to help them in any way I could. As a result of this urgent six-week project, our product's final test yields improved immensely and they were steady. Our Japanese supplier's ceramic magnetic recording head sales doubled.

LESSONS LEARNED FROM THIS PROJECT EVENT

- Degradation of crucial production parameters such as the final product test yield can be traced all the way to your subcontractor's processes.
- You have to do all you can to help your subcontractor to find and correct manufacturing problems that are affecting your final product yields.

Case 5.9: Listening to an Engine Assembler

I was a senior scientist on a team of five engineers and two designers. We designed from the ground up a 70 HP at 5000 RPM rotary engine for compact cars. The design was completed in one year and we contracted a British firm to build the engine prototypes. We were bench testing the first prototype engine. During test runs from cold start, the oil pressure was always showing high and exceeding the preset limit. Initially, we thought that there was a design flow in some of the oil passages in the engine. We did some investigative work, but we could not pin down where the problem was. My team's engineers, including myself, were pulling our hair out trying to determine the cause of this malfunction.

One of the engine assemblers, named Freddie, thought that the oil pressure relief valve exit hole that dumps excess pressure oil directly back into the oil sump was too small in diameter. He showed me the relief hole and insisted from his experience with other similar engines that it should be larger in diameter. I listened to his constructive input and went to the project manager to inform him about the observation from the engine assembler. I asked the project manager if we should repeat the oil exit hole sizing calculations to see if there was an error in them that we missed.

The project manager agreed with me and asked one of our engineers to repeat the oil pressure relief valve exit hole sizing calculations. He asked me to be the checker for the new calculations. The oil flow velocity equation that was used initially in high oil pressure cases was wrong and during these initial calculations we predicted higher velocities in small diameter holes. Our new calculations with the correct oil flow velocity equation predicted that the required oil pressure relief valve exit hole diameter be doubled. We changed all the required drawings and released them for the next set of engines to be built. We also modified the existing engines. The updated engines ran with great performance even in cold weather conditions without exceeding the preset oil pressure limit.

I went back to Freddie and thanked him for his valuable advice and asked him and his wife to join us for dinner at an exclusive restaurant in the city. He was very grateful. We had a great time in celebrating Freddie's constructive input to our project.

Listening to the engine assembler saved us precious time in finding the solution to a simple nagging malfunction in our engines. These types of events happen many times during the life of a project. Listening to your customer's input, to your subcontractor's input, to the regulatory agency input, to input from people around you from secretaries to assemblers might save your project. Listening to all input and filtering it down to useful ones for your project is an art in itself. As a project manager, you have to be appreciative of all input, good or bad, and you should not forget to reward the good ones.

LESSONS LEARNED FROM THIS PROJECT EVENT

- A nagging problem can be solved easily by listening to others.
- As project managers, we have to be very open-minded to ideas and suggestions given by others. Our easygoing and appreciative attitude will encourage everyone around us to sound their input for the goodness of our project.

Case 5.10: Russian Federation Technical Passport Issue

Bureaucracy was a major hurdle in shipping equipment to a project for a Russian Federation oil platform. As a part of the project, technical passports were required to ship our equipment to Russia. The Russian Federation regulatory authorities review and approve the equipment documents ahead of shipment. They issue a GOST-R certificate of conformity for customs clearance. I had to send all the equipment drawings, specification sheets, quality and conformity certificates, certificates of origin, and operating manuals in Russian to the Russian authorities about three months before the shipment. That would give them enough time for their review and for a question and answer period and to release the certificate of conformity.

I estimated that all the documents that had to be submitted to be around 1,000 pages. I got bids from two agencies that were experts in obtaining these certificates. These agencies do all the translation into Russian, submit the documents, do the follow-up and resolve all the conflicts, and get the certificate in time before shipment of our equipment. These agencies asked $60,000 to do the entire job. This expense was not funded in our original bidding for the project. We had to spend this amount from our margin. My upper management asked me to look into other ways of obtaining the Russian Federation certificate. I researched and found a certified Russian technical translator for $15 per page. If we got our documents translated and submitted them ourselves, we would increase our margin by $45,000.

I went to my management and explained to them the alternate way of getting the certificate of conformity. We all agreed to submit our documents to the Russian Federation regulatory authorities ourselves. I got all the documents translated into Russian, which took two months. I sent all the documents by FedEx three months before the shipment to the Russian Federation regulatory authorities.

I followed up the approval process by e-mail and by telephone with my Russian translator next to me every week. We always received an answer from a secretary that our documents were in the review cycle and we should get the approval any day. A month had passed and I started to get edgy. Two months passed and we got the same response, that the review cycle was almost complete. I could not wait anymore. I had only one month to ship our equipment according to our contract with our customer. I talked with my customer's project manager about the runaround I was getting from the regulatory authorities in Russia. He warned me that their response was typical. He advised me that I should have gone with an expert agency to get the certificate of conformity. These agencies knew how to push the paperwork and get the certificate of conformity on time.

I immediately contacted one of the agencies I had dealt with before. I got a new bid from them to obtain the certificate of conformity in a month with all documents already in Russian. This time I received a $40,000 price tag. I went to my upper management and laid out the details and the risks to them. We decided not to wait anymore. We had to go with the expert agency to obtain the certificate of conformity. These agencies had offices in Moscow and they hand carried all the documents and followed their progress daily. If there was a hiccup they took care of it right there. They promised to obtain the certificate of conformity within a month and I received it by overnight FedEx two days before our equipment shipment.

After all this hoopla, I made an extra $5,000 in our margin, but it was not worth it. I had several sleepless nights and spent a lot of my time following a Russian Federation regulatory authority process, which I had no control over. I should have put my foot down with my upper management and should have gone with an expert agency from the beginning of the process.

I received the certificate of conformity for my original application four months later by mail. Bureaucracy in a foreign government can hurt your project in many ways. You have to go along with the experts to solve your problems with the bureaucrats even if it costs your project an arm and a leg.

LESSONS LEARNED FROM THIS PROJECT EVENT

- Let certified people or companies handle government bureaucracies in foreign countries.
- Do not cut corners to reduce your cost when dealing with foreign governments.

Case 5.11: Natural Disaster Insurance

We were contracted to design, build, and install communication equipment in a gas pipeline in Bangladesh. We prepared and tested all subassemblies of the equipment in our facilities. Then we packaged them in waterproof crates and shipped them using land/ocean/land routes to their destination. We had a reliable freight forwarder who insured the goods that were being shipped against all risks of physical loss or damage for door-to-door transportation. All risks cargo insurance covered damages during loading and unloading, all transportation, war, strikes, riots, civil commotion, theft, and nondelivery of any portion of the shipment. Our cargo insurance even covered jettisoning of containers during the voyage in the ocean that could be encountered due to adverse conditions.

The total cargo insurance cost for all the equipment that filled up two 40-foot containers was over $60,000. The shipment was scheduled to arrive at the port of Chittagong, Bangladesh in five weeks. At the beginning of the fifth week, I received an e-mail from our freight forwarder that the shipment had arrived at the port of Chittagong and our containers were unloaded successfully. I got ready to send my engineering team to Bangladesh for the installation process.

One of my engineers informed me that there was a cyclone forming in the Bay of Bengal and it was heading north toward Bangladesh. I immediately called our freight forwarder regarding the status of our two containers at the port. He assured me that he would talk to his agent in Bangladesh and get the two containers transported inland away from the cyclone hit areas of the coast. He also told me that our all risk insurance did not cover natural disasters. That was very disturbing news to me. Apparently, we had to buy separate insurance coverage for natural disasters such as earthquakes, cyclones, flooding, and so on. To save us around $10,000 our shipping department and our freight forwarder decided to bypass the natural disaster insurance for my project's equipment. I was very worried at that point. I called my manager and the company president and explained to them the pickle we were in. Then I called my customer to warn them about the status of their equipment shipment with the upcoming massive storm and our lack of insurance coverage for natural disasters.

I could do nothing, but wait and pray. I was hoping that my freight forwarders agent in Bangladesh could move our containers inland before the cyclone hit land. I started to follow the cyclone news on the Internet. It was a massive and powerful cyclone packing heavy rains and destructive winds. It was heading toward the Indian and Bangladesh coastlines. Satellite images showed the cyclone's spinning tails covering a huge area. Weather forecasters predicted the storm to make landfall the next day near the border between India and Bangladesh.

I could not sleep that night. I followed the storm very closely. There was no news from our freight forwarder regarding our two containers' whereabouts. The next morning I saw on the news that the cyclone had made landfall closer to the Indian shoreline. Chittagong and its vicinity got hit by heavy rains and 100-mph winds. At 8 a.m., I received a call from our freight forwarder that our two containers were still at the Chittagong port. They could not move them inland due to the storm. Our two containers were under 3 feet of water. Luckily, our equipment was very well packaged and all weather protected. The cyclone had a large footprint, but only its tail hit the port of Chittagong. We came very close to losing all of our equipment.

As a project manager, I should have questioned in detail the insurance coverage of my shipment. When I heard that we had all risk insurance, I did not dig into further detail. That was a mistake. My team, my management, my customer, my freight forwarder, and myself had a very scary 36 hours. I wished we had the extra coverage for natural disasters. What we went through was not at all worth the $10,000 saved.

LESSONS LEARNED FROM THIS PROJECT EVENT

- As project managers, we have to cover and ask smart questions about every segment of our project. We cannot leave any unturned stone that might come back and bite us at the end.
- Saving a little money in a large project is not worth the trouble and the agony you have to go through.

Case 5.12: Project Partners

Bidding for a project can get quite complicated. You have to strengthen your company's position in a bidding war by partnering with other companies in order to have a winning chance. In a project you might partner with another company or companies for financial reasons, for technical reasons, for domestic content reasons (in international bids), and for rules and regulations coverage reasons. Project management can get complicated in a multicompany team environment. You have to have the responsibilities of each party well defined. You have to have a well-agreed-upon pecking order for project management authority.

In a volume production project to build an advanced passenger vehicle, a complex team of international companies agreed to participate in a start-up automotive company. I performed a detailed feasibility study for the volume production project. Design of the vehicle was completed by the start-up company and the vehicle's manufacturing was in the prototype phase. In volume production, the vehicle's unibody frame construction was going to be manufactured in Italy by a well-known automotive company. The drivetrain was going to be supplied by a well-respected French automotive company. The final assembly and test of the vehicle were going to be done in a new volume production plant in the United States by the start-up automotive company. The project was being financed by a couple of high-powered venture capital investors in the United States. It took about a year of negotiations to bring all involved companies together as a team and to sign final contracts. The technical project partners and financial project partners were all on solid ground. Everyone was upbeat for a successful project.

The project manager of the whole project, a good friend of mine, formed three separate project teams, one in Italy, one in France, and one in the United States. Every team had well-defined project tasks, project schedules, and a team leader who reported to him. The project manager had to travel a lot between three project groups to coordinate and be up to date regarding every task. This project was in the 1980s, and Internet communication was just starting and international calling systems were not as good. You had to be on location in order to assess the true status of a project. The project's manager had to present cost performance analysis of the project to financing groups on a weekly basis. Final assembly and test facilities for volume production were near completion after a year. During that time, 60 prototypes of the advanced passenger vehicle were built and tested thoroughly and successfully.

Everything for the volume production project was going as planned. The first vehicle was scheduled to roll out of the volume production line in January of 1988. However, stock markets around the world crashed all of a sudden in October of 1987. Financial backers of the project had to drop out of the project with their losses. Efforts to raise additional capital to get the project moving were fruitless in that financial turmoil. At the end of 1987, operations at the new start-up automotive company came to a halt. The project manager did a heck of a job for three years to bring this highly complicated multinational project to the gates of volume production, but his luck ran out as a result of an unforeseen financial crisis.

In another project, I was leading a project team to design, build, manufacture, test, and install high-pressure hydraulic cylinders in a very low temperature environment. My company had to team up with a seal manufacturer in Germany during the bidding phase of the contract. The German company was responsible for designing, manufacturing, and delivering to us special cylinder seals. The German company's technical know-how was in designing and manufacturing high-pressure seals operated in very cold temperatures. The German company brought a good technical boost to the winning bid combination. The German company had a well-defined responsibility, a schedule, and a project team. They were supposed to deliver the first articles in six months. The project was progressing on schedule. At the end of the fourth month, there was a shuffle in the German project team without my approval. The new team members were novices and they started to delay their seal delivery dates. The special seals were constantly failing very low-temperature life tests. I started to get worried.

I met with my company's president and explained the alarming situation to him. We decided to send our quality manager immediately to Germany to evaluate our project's progress on-site. His project status reports to me were not favorable at all. This private and small German company was going through an upper management shake-up. They had lost several of their experienced designers. The quality manager's recommendation was to drop the German company and to find another partner for designing and manufacturing special seals for our hydraulic cylinders. I discussed this emergency situation with my company's president. We decided together to cancel our seal project partnership with the German company because of their failure to fulfill our joint contract commitments. We could go this route only after getting an okay from my customer's project manager. My customer's project manager agreed with my proposal to change our German partner. My purchasing department and I scrambled to find another seal company that could design and provide us special seals in an expedited schedule. Luckily, we found one close to our facilities in the United States. My customer's project manager and I visited our new seal design and manufacturing partner for qualification. The qualification visit was very successful. We signed a contract with our new special seal design and manufacturing partner in one week. I monitored their progress very closely. I also had one of my project team engineers reside at the new seal company for the duration of the whole project. When everything was said and done, my company was late one month in delivering our hydraulic cylinders to our customer's site. However, I was very lucky to be able to turn around the special seal crisis.

At the bidding phase of a project, all project partners look eager and willing to win the bid. Many unforeseen issues might surface with our project partners during the execution phase of the project. As project managers, it is our responsibility to remedy these project partner issues as fast as we can without damaging the cost and schedule performance of our project.

LESSONS LEARNED FROM THIS PROJECT EVENT

- In a multicompany partnership project environment, there has to be a mutually agreed upon project manager who is responsible for the whole project.
- You have to be proactive and drop some of your project partners in a timely fashion if they are not performing up to par.

Case 5.13: Cost Overrun Due to Steel Price Increase

I was heading a project to design, build, and test 20 high-load capacity and high-pressure hydraulic cylinders for a customer in Brazil. Each cylinder was priced at $200k. The total project revenue was $4M. Each cylinder's cost was broken down to distributed design costs, manufacturing costs, and testing, which was $120k per cylinder. Material costs for each cylinder were $40k. Packaging and shipment of the cylinders were the customer's responsibility, namely, delivery was ex-factory. So each cylinder would have a cost of $160k with a total project cost of $3.2M, which resulted in a project margin of 20%.

The material cost was mainly the special steel cost used in building the hydraulic cylinders. We could only use steel from the customer's qualified countries and qualified suppliers in those countries. My purchasing agent was screening all the qualified steel manufacturing suppliers and dealers. Due to a large demand for steel from China, steel prices skyrocketed during my project, which we did not account for in our pricing. With high steel prices our material costs were going to increase by 50% to $60k for each cylinder. This unexpected cost increase in steel would have lowered our project margins to 10%. I had a meeting with my team and with my upper management to brainstorm the skyrocketing price of steel for my project. One of the vice presidents suggested that I should discuss this issue with our customer's project manager too. Our customer had large steel construction projects. Maybe purchasing our steel under our customer's umbrella would give us some relief in price.

After our internal meeting, I immediately sent an e-mail to our customer's project manager to set up a teleconference with him regarding our project's steel costs. During the teleconference, I told him that we were going to get a big hit to our project margin with the current steel prices. We discussed several ways to solve the high steel pricing issue at hand. He promised to look into the matter in his company to see if they could help us in any way. They also purchased a lot of steel themselves for their other projects. Our customer's project manager got back to me in a week with exciting news. He said that they just qualified a new steel vendor in South Africa. They were ready to purchase a substantial amount of steel for themselves for another project. He discussed our high steel price issue with his material purchasing manager. His material purchasing manager agreed to piggyback us onto his order in order for us to get a reasonable discount. His material purchasing manager was leaving for South Africa in two days to finalize his steel order. I proposed that I send my purchasing agent along with him so that we could get steel for my project at a reasonable price by riding on their coattails. Our customer's project manager and their purchasing manager were very understanding and helpful in accepting my proposal.

My purchasing agent traveled to South Africa with our customer's purchasing manager. After a couple of days of negotiations, together they negotiated a good deal for us with the new South African steel supplier. We only had to pay $8k extra for each cylinder's steel. This steel supplier was also able to provide the steel in a timely manner for my project with the required material certificates. I was lucky that I was able to piggyback my project's special steel order with my customer's substantial steel purchase order. This deal was quite a success story for my project during continually rising steel prices. It saved our project's margin from going down to 10%. With this new South African steel deal, our project's margin eroded down to a reasonable value of 16%.

I was elated with the help I received from our customer on this steel deal. I sent our customer's project manager and his purchasing manager two bottles of fine whisky for their excellent support in helping us to get my project's steel at a very reasonable price. I also gave my purchasing agent a dinner gift certificate for two at a restaurant of his choice.

I kept my upper management informed continually about the status of the South African steel deal. They were very happy about the final steel deal. I asked the president of my company to write a thank you letter to the president of our customer while praising the help we got from our customer's project manager and from their purchasing agent in our steel deal. Teamwork like this went a long way in making a project a success in a win-win situation.

LESSONS LEARNED FROM THIS PROJECT EVENT

- An unexpected rise in material costs during the execution of a project will bite into your company's profit margin.
- It is a good practice to lock down material costs at the beginning of a project without any delay before surprise increases hit your project.

Case 5.14: Actual Cost of Work Performance

As the project manager I had to keep track of the schedule performance index and cost performance index for every task group.

I presented these two important schedule performance and cost performance indices to upper management every two weeks or at most every four weeks. Schedule performance indices were easier to calculate because input to work completion estimates were determined by me and task groups. However, it was very difficult to obtain input for cost performance indices.

I had to chase our accounting department every month in order to be able to collect all costs charged to my project's charge numbers. The accounting department was always late in getting all charges collected. They also made unthinkable mistakes. I saw many charges from unrelated company personnel to my project. I saw several equipment costs charged to my project by mistake or knowingly. At the end of every fiscal month, defined as four weeks, four weeks, and five weeks, I had to get these erroneous charges cleaned up before I could determine the actual cost of the work performed by every task group of my project.

I expressed my concerns about delays and errors occurring in the accounting department to my manager. My manager set up a meeting with the chief financial officer. During the meeting, I voiced my concerns with examples. I emphasized that my project was a very dynamic one with a tight budget. I had to know the charges made to my project's charge numbers, 14 of them, at most within a week from the end of the fiscal month. I asked them to allow me to sit down with the accounting department's personnel at the end of every fiscal month to go over all the charges made to my project's account numbers. The chief financial officer agreed to my requests and promised to improve cost reporting delays and errors.

One month passed yet the situation with cost accounting did not improve. Two months passed and it was the same old story. I had to get my project's cost accounting fixed. I, myself, made an appointment with the chief executive officer of the company and laid in front of him the details of our company's cost accounting delays and errors. He told me that he was aware of the slow pace of our accounting department in preparing the fiscal monthly cost report. I told him that I could not fulfill my project management duties in a timely manner and take the necessary steps to correct for cost overruns at this tempo. He promised me that he would discuss the accounting department issues with the chief financial officer immediately and they would make the necessary improvements to enhance the company's cost account speed and error rate.

At the end of the next fiscal month, the cost report came out in two days. There was one error in my project's cost report. I was so happy. I sent thank you e-mails to our chief financial officer and copied our chief executive officer and my manager. I was able to get the actual cost of work performed within two days after every fiscal month. I was able to balance my under budget task groups with over budget task groups and determine what actions to take to improve my project's cost estimates to completion. More often than not, my projects overran the budgeted cost of work. Then I had to present the overrun reasons to my upper management and get their okay to dip into my project's contingency funds or dip into the company's company margin.

There was another major issue with the project cost accounting, which was the timely submission of travel expense reports. My team members filed their expense reports within a week of their return to home base. However, some manufacturing department engineers and some quality department engineers submitted their trip expense reports one to six months late. I had to nudge every one of them and their managers to get their trip expense reports filed with the accounting department in a timely fashion. Finally, I got tired of nudging them and took the trip expense report timely filing issue to my upper management. After a couple of discussions with upper management, it became a requirement in the company for everyone to submit their trip expense reports within one week of their arrival to home base.

Monitoring schedule and cost performances of a project very closely at regular intervals is a must for a project manager. You have to bring your company's other departments in sync with your project's dynamic environment. The challenge is to be able to collect all schedule and cost performance data in a timely fashion from your foreign project partners.

LESSONS LEARNED FROM THIS PROJECT EVENT

- Your project's cost performance can be hampered by your finance department's delays and errors.
- A trip expense report for a project should be filed and approved within a week of completion.
- Periodically always check every item charged to your project.

6

CASE STUDIES IN TEAM MANAGEMENT

Every team member of your project has a different personality and behavior. You are a mentor, a role model, and a psychologist to all your team members.

Stability in the lives of the project team's members helps tremendously to run a project smoothly. I had to help a troubled team member straighten out his family issues as outlined in Case 6.1.

A senior scientist's adverse behavior affected my team's morale and started to hamper the progress of my project. I had to take serious steps to bring him in line so that my project could progress smoothly. Case 6.2 outlines the steps that I had to take in order to bring harmony into my project team.

Errors are part of real life in engineering projects. They can happen in design, in a customer's specifications, in manufacturing, in quality control, in receiving inspections, at subcontractors, at certification laboratories, and so on. The key is to catch them in a timely fashion. Hopefully, the error will only cause a minor distraction to the project. If everyone involved with the project can learn from the mistake made, you will be making a big contribution to your company as a project manager. Such an encounter is detailed in Case 6.3.

To execute a project in a foreign country can be very challenging. It helps a lot in the progress and success of your project if you and your team members are immersed in the foreign country's traditions and language. In Case 6.4, my team had to be trained on the ins and outs of Japanese business culture and business language.

In one of my projects, a senior engineer on my team decided to take a three-month sabbatical leave from the company right in the middle of the project. He was a crucial member of my team. These kinds of unexpected situations can arise in any project. As the project manager, my task was to find a remedy to this crisis fast without hampering the progress of my project as described in Case 6.5.

Traveling to foreign countries for a job can be very strenuous. It requires detailed preparation. Passport issues, visa issues, money issues, security issues, language differences, hotels, transportation, and foreign contacts all have to be dealt with in utmost detail and accuracy ahead of a trip. As project managers, it is our responsibility to make sure that all the i's are dotted and all the t's are crossed before a foreign trip is made as shown in Case 6.6.

Nonperforming and/or underperforming team members are always an issue during the life of a project. Keeping them on the team or getting rid of them has to be weighed very carefully. Risk analysis of your actions has to be thought out in utmost detail. The effects of an underperforming team member can be very destructive in a dynamic team environment. Such a situation is detailed in Case 6.7.

One of the important tasks of a project manager is to attend special ceremonies involving your team members. These ceremonies can be birthday parties, weddings, patent presentation banquets, technical society presentations, and so forth. As a team leader one of your main functions is to participate in your team member's celebration events. Such an international event is detailed in Case 6.8.

A work environment should be like a second family environment away from home. Every employee should be able to talk and express his or her issues and concerns to their managers, upper management, and/or to human resources without any reservations or fears. These issues and concerns can be personal ones, work-related ones, or community-related ones. As managers, our responsibility is to help every employee as much as we can to make them feel that they are always under our company's family umbrella as described in Case 6.9.

In a project environment, during the course of events, several unexpected sacrifices can come from any one of your team members. Sometimes these sacrifices can come from people outside of your team. As the project manager, you have to recognize and appreciate these kinds of above and beyond duties. Such an example is detailed in Case 6.10.

I have seen many project teams go through a honeymoon period at the beginning or at the middle of a project throughout my career. As project managers, we have to watch for slacking signs from every team member and take the necessary action to keep the pressure cooker at a constant stress level. An unfortunate slacking period is detailed in Case 6.11.

When a good employee who helped you a lot in your project is leaving the company, you have to provide a memorable farewell to him or her. I managed to give a great farewell party to my senior mechanical tool designer when expenses were very restricted in my company as detailed in Case 6.12.

As I gained experience in project management, I only made promises that I could keep to my team members. I researched thoroughly beforehand, if I could keep my promise. When I gave a time frame for a promise, I always accomplished it within that time frame as depicted in Case 6.13.

Several unexpected events can occur during the course of a project. Some project managers get upset and blow their tops, but this type of behavior does not solve anything. Negative reactions make things worse. You have to be coolheaded, versatile, and firm to find other solutions fast in order to bring the difficult situation at hand under control as shown in Case 6.14.

As project managers, we have to sometimes act as psychologists. We should not take drastic actions on a whim or with a burst of anger. We have to consider all repercussions that an immediate action might cause in our project as shown in Case 6.15.

Specialists and/or scientists can be very moody and demanding in a team environment. As a project manager, you need their expertise. You have to treat them with respect. You have to create a flexible boundary with their needs and with your project's requirements. If you become a hard-liner with such people, your project will suffer in the end as shown in Case 6.16.

A project's work atmosphere can be very different after a personal vacation or after holidays. As project managers, we have to settle down anxiety or lackadaisical behavior after such events as detailed in Case 6.17.

Maternity leave can be very disrupting to a project's progress. As project managers, we have to work with our human resources department in order to make the right decisions and appropriate arrangements to solve the issues at hand as detailed in Case 6.18.

As project managers, we have to encourage and empower our team members constantly to make improvement suggestions to their tasks. Such improvement suggestions can come from unexpected sources. We have to praise and reward contributing suggestions to our project as detailed in Case 6.19.

Efficiently run meetings are the backbone of a project. Meetings have to be standardized and managed properly so that team members' precious time is not wasted. A team member should not be bored and he or she should contribute constructively while present during a project meeting. Especially in large team groups, as it was in Case 6.20, breaking up a meeting into smaller subgroups can be very effective.

Mishaps happen more often than not while preparing for critical meetings or deadlines in a project. Overworked and overtired team members become prone to mistakes and accidents. As project managers, we have to watch over our team members and over ourselves for fatigue and for burnout conditions as detailed in Case 6.21.

Case 6.1: Getting a Senior Wafer Fabrication Engineer's Life Stabilized

The project was to set up a new 6″ wafer fabrication for computer disk drive heads into production. I had an engineer assigned to every piece of equipment in the new wafer factory. They were tasked for sourcing the equipment, qualifying the equipment, and optimizing that particular equipment's process for the computer disk drive head specifications using design of experiments. The project was fast paced with a duration of six months.

One of the senior engineers in charge of the nickel iron plating module was starting to slack off and he was falling behind in his tasks. He was the owner of the nickel iron plating module. He wrote the specifications for it. He sourced the manufacturer. He went to North Carolina to accept the module. He was now performing design of experiments to optimize the pulsed power supply, current density, bath temperature, and agitation of the electrolyte solution for critical nickel iron parameters.

I went to his office and started to discuss the delays in his tasks and asked him if he needed any help to catch up. He said he had some family issues and he was certain that he would be able to complete the design of experiments in time and qualify the nickel iron plating module. A week passed. I sensed that things were not progressing smoothly. This plating engineer was under a lot of stress. I called him to my office and started to have a heart-to-heart discussion about his missed commitments. He started to open up and explain to me his family issues. His wife left him and they were going through a divorce. During this turmoil, his 12-year-old son was staying with him. He had to run every day and take him to school and back from school. He was trying to sell his house. The poor guy was ready to flip due to extreme stress. I asked him if I could be of any help. I told him to think about it. I did not want to lose him at this juncture of the project and bring in a new engineer from the cold. I asked him if we could have lunch together that day. He said okay.

Until lunchtime I made a couple of telephone calls to human resources and I saw my supervisor to find out if the company could provide him a company-owned apartment for the next six months. I explained my senior engineer's situation in confidence and how it was affecting my project. I received favorable responses from all sources. He did not have to pay any rent and the company apartments were very close to his son's school.

We had a heart-to-heart discussion about his family situation during our lunch. I told him about the company's apartment offer. He was very appreciative and accepted it. I asked him if there was anything else I could help him with in order to stabilize his family life. He told me that he was looking for a good divorce lawyer. I told him that I would investigate finding a good divorce lawyer for him through our legal department. I emphasized to him the importance of his work for the start-up of the 6″ wafer factory. I also emphasized to him to come to me if he ran into any other difficult hurdles.

I had to walk a fine line when I dealt with this troubled senior engineer. I wanted to help him all I could without becoming too friendly with him and without losing his respect for me. Getting sucked into non-work-related issues with a team member can be very tricky for a project manager. I had to go along with the company rules and regulations. I would not promise him something that I could not deliver. Above all, my project's health was my main concern.

I went to our legal department and discussed the divorce lawyer issue with the company's head legal counselor. He called a divorce lawyer friend of his in town and arranged a meeting with my senior engineer. The two met and agreed on terms. The senior engineer was very grateful to me. On top of everything, he got a substantially reduced rate from the divorce lawyer.

In two days time, the senior engineer moved into the company's apartment. He signed his son up for an afterschool program so that he did not have to rush to school in the middle of the afternoon. His performance at work improved instantly. He put in some extra hours and finished his tasks only one week late.

As a project manager, I was very gratified that I could help a troubled member of my team. Other options such as replacing the team member in the critical segment of a project or assigning another junior engineer to help him could have been more risky.

Identifying risky areas in a project should be a continual task for a project manager. After a risky situation is identified, you should identify various paths to cure the risky situation. You should choose the path that you as the project manager can have the most control over. Risk management in a controlled fashion is very crucial to a project's success.

LESSONS LEARNED FROM THIS PROJECT EVENT

- As project managers, we have to be good psychologists too.
- Identifying and dealing with a team member's stress level and risky condition are our number one responsibility as project managers.
- Helping a project team member to get on track in his or her personal life is very gratifying.

Case 6.2: A Recalcitrant Engineer on a Project Team

I was asked to develop the next generation of thin film magnetic heads with a team of four physicists and electrical engineers in one year in order to keep ahead of the competition. The magnetic head design had to be very efficient and increase the areal density of magnetic recording at least an order of magnitude. I had a very bright and innovative group on my team. The team was given to me and I did not have any say in picking the team members.

We started the project on a very positive footing. After a week, one of the prominent members of the team started spreading negative rumors about the company and he was not attending some of our team meetings. He came to work late and left work as he pleased. He had a Ph.D. in physics from MIT and he behaved like a disobedient child. His behavior affected my team's morale and started to hamper the progress of my project.

I called him to my office and had a heart-to-heart discussion with him about his attitude. I told him that he was a very valuable member of my team and we depended on his magnetic design calculations and recommendations. He told me he was what he was and he did not like to work in a team environment. I asked him not to spread rumors against the company and discourage the team members and asked him to try to work with the team members as efficiently as he could. I told him I would not mind him using flexible hours at work. He agreed that he would try his best and left our meeting with good intentions.

Another week passed, but nothing had changed. His behavior got worse. He started to bring some of the other team members to his office and shut the door to have hours of discussions. I learned that these discussions were not about our project. They were discussing the stock market, who was going to make a bid to buy our company, when our company's president was going to be fired, when was a layoff going to happen, and so on. This physicist was a team breaker and not a team builder. I had to take more serious steps to bring him in line so that the project could progress smoothly.

I went to his supervisor and discussed this physicist's behavior in confidence with him. His supervisor told me that this physicist was a recalcitrant person and he did not like to be under anyone's authority, he looked down on everyone, and he thought his knowledge was superior to anyone around him. I told his supervisor that I needed this physicist's contributions to my project. I told him that I was going to control this grown up and obstinate scientist very closely so that my team could successfully complete the project.

I had a team meeting without the recalcitrant physicist. I asked my team members not to interact with this physicist. I told them that I would be the only interface between him and the team. I went over the reasons for my actions. The rest of my team members understood the delicate situation with this physicist. After the team meeting, I called the disobedient physicist to my office and explained to him that team harmony was necessary to succeed in our project. I told him that we needed his invaluable input to the project. I asked him to interface only through me regarding the project and not with the team members. I also asked him to move his office next to mine, which luckily was not occupied at the time. I asked him not to attend the team meetings. I cautioned him not to have demoralizing discussions with my team members. I told him that my actions were not to punish him, but to make the project a successful one. He reluctantly agreed to my requests.

Then I went to the human resources department and explained to the head of the human resources department the difficulties I was having with this particular employee on my team. I outlined all the actions I was taking to remedy the issue. I also emphasized that I needed this physicist's contributions for my project. She asked me to write a review letter about him and list all the actions I was taking to remedy the behavior of this physicist. I wrote a detailed review letter and discussed it with the recalcitrant physicist. I gave a copy to him. I also gave copies of my review letter to his supervisor and to the human resources department.

This obstinate physicist worked under my very close supervision for the next six months and he contributed extensively to my project. He heavily cut his demoralizing activities during these six months. I made him work in a completely isolated environment. Unfortunately, at the end of six months, he was let go during a layoff because of his behavior. He predicted the company's layoff timing right on the dot. He was a paragon of magnetism as a physicist, but he was not a team player at all.

LESSONS LEARNED FROM THIS PROJECT EVENT

- You have to take immediate action to deal with people who are disrupting your project team's harmony and who are demoralizing your project team members.
- Some high-level scientists behave like a child in a team environment. These kinds of people need to be micromanaged with very close supervision.

Case 6.3: Error in Motor Mount Moment of Inertia Calculations

I was heading a vehicle design group to design an all terrain vehicle for a German customer. The design was completed on time and approved by the customer. My company's manufacturing group was starting to build 20 vehicles for beta testing. All chassis were built and all the motor mounts were built. They were in the process of welding them together. During this juncture of the project, one of my structural engineers walked into my office with a red face and told me that he made a calculation mistake during the design of the motor mount beams. He forgot to divide the beam's moment of inertia calculation by a constant, namely by 12, and he was very sorry about it. Another structural engineer who checked his calculations also missed this moment of inertia calculation error. This error created unacceptable bending stress levels in the motor mount beams during dynamic loading.

I immediately called our manufacturing manager and asked him to put a hold on all chassis and motor mount construction. I told my structural engineer to keep cool. I told him we all make mistakes. The important thing was to learn from our mistakes and not to repeat them again. I called the calculation checker to my office. I advised him in a similar fashion. I told both of them that I would control the damage. I asked them to get together, focus, and revise the motor mount calculation and come back with relined drawings in a day. I called a team meeting to explain this unfortunate error to all team members and to discuss what steps we should take so that similar errors would not occur again.

The team meeting was very productive. I praised the structural engineer for coming forward and discovering his error in the early phase of manufacturing. The focus of the meeting was to find a better way to check our calculations so that they would be error-free. We decided to double our checkpoints for all critical calculations. One of the checkers was going to be outside the project team, namely an independent and a well-qualified checker. This new design process would add a couple of extra days to the release of calculation documents, but would give us more reliable results. The manufacturing manager and the manufacturing lead for the project were also invited to the team meeting. We discussed time and cost damages due to the design error. All 20 motor mounts were going to be scrapped. The total time lost in manufacturing would be about five days and it would cost the project an extra of $20k to build the new motor mounts. Manufacturing processes in other subassemblies would be able to move forward. These schedule and cost impacts were mild and they were recoverable.

Then I called a meeting with my manager and the structural engineers' manager. I explained the unfortunate events to the two managers. We went through my solutions. They were both satisfied with my team's solutions to the error. However, the structural engineers' manager got upset with his engineers. He was a flashy type of a person. He wanted to discipline both of them. He even leaned toward firing them. I asked him to cool down a little bit. I told him that we all make mistakes, but the key was to learn from these mistakes and not to repeat them again. I asked the structural engineers' manager not to discipline his engineers. I told him that these two engineers are very promising young ones. They needed grooming and needed a positive support from a negative event. They would contribute immensely to the company projects in years to come. I told the structural engineers' manager that the structural engineer came forward to me on his own with a red face. He was very honest and very sorry about the error he made. We were lucky to catch the error in the early phase of manufacturing. My project was going to get a minor hit, but in the end the two structural engineers would gain a real-life experience. We discussed the issue heatedly for an hour. The structural engineers' manager finally agreed with my recommendations and promised not to do anything counterproductive to discourage them.

Errors are part of real life in engineering projects. They can happen in design, in the customer's specifications, in manufacturing, in quality control, in receiving inspection, at subcontractors, at certification laboratories, and so on. The key is to catch them before the project is completed. Hopefully, the error would cause a minor distraction to the project. If everyone involved with the project could learn from the mistake made, you could make a big contribution to your company as a project manager. I have heard of several major errors made during a project too, such as in a space project when the payload of an unmanned space probe was calculated in pounds instead of kilograms.

LESSONS LEARNED FROM THIS PROJECT EVENT

- Errors are more likely to occur during the execution of a project.
- As project managers, we have to be coolheaded and make sure that our team learns from a mistake made in order not to repeat it again.
- As project managers, we have to correct errors in a timely fashion.
- As project managers, we have to gather our project team in order to explain what the error was and how we are going to take care of it.

Case 6.4: Training in the Japanese Language

My company, a customized computer component designer and manufacturer, planned to increase our market share in Japan. I was given the engineering responsibility for guiding our design and application engineers to go periodically to Japan to visit our potential customers. We had to present our future products and convince our potential customers as to how advanced our products were and how advanced and controlled our manufacturing processes were.

I went to Japan several times with my design and application engineers. We all were struggling to get to know the Japanese culture and their workplace ethics, such as how to greet people from your customer's end, how to exchange business cards, how to exchange small gifts, how to behave in a meeting, how to make small talk, how to behave at lunches and dinners, and so on. When I returned to the United States from my second visit to Japan, I decided that we should be trained in the Japanese business culture and language. I requested a meeting with my company's president regarding the necessary training, if we wanted to succeed in business in Japan.

My company president was very receptive to my training idea in the Japanese business culture and language. He further proposed that this training should be a requirement for all of our employees who dealt with Japan. He asked me to arrange it with our human resources department. Our human resources department found a perfect trainer from the University of California. He was Japanese and he was studying for his Ph.D. degree in psychology. He came to our company every Tuesday for a year at lunchtime and trained us on the ins and outs of Japanese business culture and business language. He taught us important Japanese phrases that we could use during our encounters with our Japanese customers. He gave us recorded tapes filled with Japanese phrases so that we could practice the pronunciations at our leisure. Since Japanese is a phonetic language, we learned pronunciation of phrases with ease.

Every one of my engineers who dealt with Japan, all of our sales personnel, purchasing personnel, and even executives who dealt with Japan took this one-year training course. Brown paper bag lunches were provided by the company. There were 26 trainees in the class. We had written and oral examinations once a month. Fifteen of us passed the course with flying colors including all of my engineers who dealt with Japan. Ten of us flunked the course and one dropped out because of health reasons.

The course taught us a lot of small talk phrases and greeting phrases in Japanese. We learned greeting phrases such as "pleased to meet you" (*hajimemashite*), "good morning" (*ohayo gozaimasu*), and "thank you very much" (*domo arigato gozaimasu*). We learned the telephone hello response, which was *moshi moshi*. At the end of a long meeting in Japan, it was customary to write down action items on the board with the names of owners and due dates. After everyone agreed on the action items list, the scriber of meeting minutes sent the action items list to everyone involved by e-mail. Once, at the end of a 12-hour meeting, I started the action items list by writing "action items" in Japanese Kanji characters on the board. All of our Japanese colleagues almost dropped out of their chairs. They had a good laugh at the end of a long and strenuous meeting.

We learned how to sit in pecking order around a conference table. As guests, our team always sat on the side of the table that was away from the conference room entrance door. We learned when to talk during a meeting. The highest-ranking member of our team always answered their questions. If that ranking member needed help from other members of his team, he mentioned that so and so would be responding to their particular question. Dinners were less formal, but again high-ranking members of both teams sat at the ends of the dinner table. A 12-hour meeting from 9 a.m. to 9 p.m. and afterward a 3-hour business dinner until midnight was a normal day in Japan.

The one-year business culture training course for Japan helped my company to gain ground in their marketplace. After two years, we saw a 10-fold sales increase for our products in Japan. The president of my company thanked me for suggesting the Japanese business culture classes for our people. Also, everyone who took the course was very appreciative for gaining such an eye-opening experience into Japanese culture and language.

LESSONS LEARNED FROM THIS PROJECT EVENT

- Every member of your team dealing with a foreign country has to know that foreign country's history, culture, and workplace ethics.
- Knowing the business language of a foreign country that you are dealing with goes a long way in negotiations and in gaining mutual respect among players.

Case 6.5: A Project Engineer Left the Company under Adverse Conditions

When I started a project with a team, I made sure that I had all the information about each team member's vacation plans, wedding and honeymoon plans, and other time-off plans. I put every team member's personal time-off plan into the project schedule and I made sure that there were no conflicts with project tasks and deliverables.

In one of my projects, a senior engineer on my team decided to take a three-month sabbatical leave from the company right in the middle of the project. He was a crucial member of my team. He was doing dynamic stress analysis for the product we were designing. He asked me to have a meeting together with his manager. During the meeting, he explained that he was an avid cyclist. He was invited to train with a cycling team and to enter an international race with this cycling team. He requested a three-month sabbatical leave starting in two weeks. This was quite a shock to me. I told them that it was not possible for him to leave my project at that critical juncture. There was no one else in the company who could step in and take over his tasks. He insisted that he had to take three months off from work, he had already made a commitment to his cycling team, and no one could stop him. I was upset with his irresponsible behavior. I told him that his first responsibility should have been to the project which he was an important part of. He should have first consulted with us before making a commitment to his cycling team. He should have told us his sabbatical leave intentions four months ago when the project started. He understood that he was not going to get anywhere with me. So he said to his manager that he wanted to give his two-week resignation notice and leave the company. He immediately left his manager's office without saying goodbye.

His manager was very upset too with his engineer's childish and obstinate behavior. He called the human resources department in front of me and explained to them the unfortunate situation. The human resources director immediately went over to the senior engineer's office to discuss if there was a way out of this quagmire. She reported to the senior engineer's manager and to me that there was no solution to the senior engineer's adamant request. They decided to walk him out the door at the end of the day without any delay. I was able to salvage some of the modeling and test runs he had done for my project before he left for good.

I had to scramble to find a replacement for my team's dynamic stress analyzer. I had a design review coming up in two months with the customer and my team had to finish all the pertinent calculations and designs before the phase 1 review meeting. To find a replacement engineer with a similar skill set would have taken at least two to three months. A novice engineer right out of college would not be able to help me. I needed an experienced mechanical engineer in stress analysis. Even if we had to steal one from another company, it would have been awhile to get him or her to be productive on my team. The only solution was to go out and find a consulting firm in dynamic stress analysis and bring them on board for my project.

I went to a couple of prominent stress analysis companies in the United States and interviewed them for my project. They were expensive. I did not have any contingency funds in my budget to cover these unexpected extra costs. I started to look at the possibilities outside the United States. I found a stress analysis company in India and one in the United Kingdom. I interviewed them by teleconferencing. I also checked their references. I made sure that they were using the same version of the stress analysis software as we used in house. The stress analysis company in the United Kingdom had the right expertise to help my project. Their price was in the middle between the U.S. and Indian companies. I went to my manager and discussed my search results with him and I told him that I was going to sign a contract with the UK subcontractor to complete my project's dynamic stress analysis requirements. He was pleased that I was able to find a potential candidate in a week. He assured me that the company would absorb the extra cost of the UK subcontractor in the project margin. My purchasing department and I completed the subcontract agreement with the UK subcontractor in three days. They started to work on my team two weeks after the senior engineer's departure.

I did all the communication by teleconferencing with the UK subcontractor. They came up to speed fast. They also worked 60 to 70 hours per week without charging me overtime. I was able to get all the required calculations and designs completed in two months time before the phase 1 review. I did not inform my customer about this crisis we had because this crisis was totally an internal issue and it did not affect the progress of the project. I resolved this crisis without disturbing my customer's project manager.

These kinds of unexpected situations can arise in any project. As the project manager, my task was to find a remedy to this crisis fast without hampering the progress of my project.

LESSONS LEARNED FROM THIS PROJECT EVENT

- As project managers, we have to make sure that at the beginning of a project, we have all the information about each team member's vacation plans, wedding and honeymoon plans, and other time-off plans on our project schedule.

- A team member's work plan can change suddenly, which can affect your project's progress adversely.
- Replacing a specialized and experienced engineer is very difficult at a moment's notice.

Case 6.6: On-Site Equipment Training

One of the requirements of building and installing a hydraulic mover on an oil platform project was to train the customer's personnel on-site. As the project manager of the project, I decided to send a senior engineer for this training. The training was in the North East region of Russia and it was for two weeks in April. April was supposed to be the beginning of spring weather in that region. My senior engineer prepared an extensive MS PowerPoint presentation for the training. He got his laptop computer and his thermal underwear and left for this cold region of Russia in early April.

He was to connect with our company's liaison in Vladivostok and then travel together to the oil platform site. My engineer did not speak a word of Russian, but our company's liaison was going to help translate his training presentations. The training was supposed to be done with two groups of 10 personnel who did not speak or understand a word of English. All the meeting dates and locations in Vladivostok with the company liaison were arranged and confirmed by Internet correspondence. My engineer arrived at the airport. During passport control the agent asked him why he was entering Russia. My engineer honestly said that he would be training 20 Russian workers on an oil platform. The agent emphasized that my engineer did not have the proper visa to enter Russia for training purposes. On top of that, his passport expiration date was within six months of his exit date. His passport expiration date should have been six months beyond his exit date from Russia. My engineer started to plead that he was there for only two weeks to help the Russian workers get trained on crucial equipment at an oil platform. The passport control agent took my engineer to a small cubicle with a glass enclosure and called his supervisor who spoke a little English. My engineer pleaded his case to the supervisor. They together tried to call our company's liaison in town, who was not to be found at work or home. The supervisor threatened to send him out of the country with the next international flight, asked him to stay put, and left the cubicle. My engineer waited in the cubicle for three hours and finally the supervisor showed up again with smiles. He told him that he discussed his situation with authorities in Moscow and they decided that he could enter Russia for only two weeks as a tourist. Finally, my engineer said, "Let me be a tourist for two weeks in your country." Then they shook hands and his passport was stamped with the tourist entry date.

My engineer took a taxi downtown to our company liaison's office. He found a secretary there who did not speak any English. They were able to communicate with hand motions and by writing. Finally, my engineer understood that our company's liaison was out of the country in South Korea for a two-day trip. Our company's liaison never informed us about the change in his plans. My engineer decided to stay in Vladivostok for two days and wait for the company liaison's return. He checked into a boutique hotel close to the company liaison's office and called me to detail all the hurdles that he crossed when he arrived in Russia. I agreed with him that he should wait for two days for the company's liaison before traveling to the training site because of the language barriers. I told him to hang in there and told him that I would inform our customer about the two-day delay in starting the training.

My engineer almost froze to death at the boutique hotel where he was staying. Apparently, the hotel personnel turned off the heat at night from 9 p.m. to 7 a.m. to save on fuel costs. The poor guy had to buy extra blankets to keep warm at night. He started to check out after two days at this freezing hotel, but his credit card bounced because his credit account was maxed out. He did not have enough cash on him to pay the hotel. He called the company's liaison office and finally he was able to touch base with the company's Russian liaison. The company's liaison came to the hotel and paid my engineer's hotel bill. My company's liaison was not even sorry that he was two days late to his appointment with my engineer.

Together they traveled by bus to a village that was 20 miles away from the oil platform. Then they took our customer's shuttle boat to the platform. They stayed on the platform for 10 days because my engineer's visa expired two days after the end of training. He had to condense his training into two five-day sessions. He could not use his laptop computer on the platform because his computer battery died. He could not charge his computer's batteries since he did not have the right adapter to the oil platform outlets. He transferred his MS PowerPoint training file to the company liaison's laptop computer and used his computer during the training sessions. It was so cold, $-20°C$, in North East Russia in April that my engineer had to sleep wearing his sweaters, pants, and alpaca socks at night. He was lucky that he did not get sick during those 10 training days. Overall the training went well. He exited Russia without any issues and made it safely back home.

I had a long meeting with him when he got back. I told him that it was my fault not to warn him about the validity of his passport duration. It was also my fault that I did not advise him on the type of visa that he should get for training purposes. He should have gotten a business visa. We discussed his credit card balance issue. He accepted that it was his fault not to straighten out his balance before he left for his trip. I went to my upper management and laid out the details of my engineer's troubles in Russia and made sure that my company cut ties with our liaison there.

Traveling to foreign countries for a job can be very strenuous. It requires detailed preparation. Passport issues, visa issues, money issues, security issues, language differences, hotels, transportation, and foreign contacts all have to be dealt with in utmost detail and accuracy ahead of a trip.

LESSONS LEARNED FROM THIS PROJECT EVENT

- As project managers, we have to be extra sure that people working for us in foreign countries are dependable.
- Before we send our team members offshore, we have to verify the validity of their travel documents.

Case 6.7: Getting Rid of a Lackadaisical Team Member

I was heading five separate groups of engineers in a wafer fabrication project. Each group had its own manager. One of the engineering groups was responsible for quality control of the incoming materials and outgoing product. There were visual inspection correlation issues regarding the outgoing wafers with our South Korean plant. My quality engineering group's manager and I decided to send one of the seasoned quality engineers to South Korea to train the South Korean engineers and inspectors per our inspection criteria. We wanted to eliminate our differences in visual inspection.

My quality engineering group's manager explained in detail to our seasoned quality engineer what his responsibilities would be in South Korea. He had two weeks to train the South Koreans and then return to his home base. He made his trip and trained the South Koreans and got back. He gave me and my quality group's manager a briefing in my office about his accomplishments in South Korea. To our surprise, he only trained the South

Koreans on one inspection parameter, which was the highest correlation discrepancy on the Pareto chart. He did not deal with any of the other inspection parameters. He made his trip and spent thousands of dollars to improve our inspection correlation only in one parameter. He overlooked all other 15 parameters which were on his checklist. I asked him why he neglected all the other inspection parameters. He responded in a spiritless manner that he had time to fix only one parameter. I asked him why he did not call his manager to discuss an extension of his stay so that he could complete his tasks fully. He said in a lackadaisical way that he felt that he completed his mission in South Korea. I politely asked the seasoned quality engineer to leave my office and complete his trip report.

I closed the door to my office and started to discuss the performance status of the seasoned quality engineer with my quality group's manager. The seasoned quality engineer had been with our company for 15 years and his performance went downhill every year. He was experienced, but he was definitely lazy. My quality group's manager did not document instances of his poor performance. His annual performance reviews were mediocre. I told my quality group's manager that this seasoned engineer would be a listless mentor for our young and dynamic engineers. I asked him if there was a way to revive the spark in work habits of the seasoned quality engineer. My quality group's manager told me he discussed the mediocre performance with the seasoned quality engineer several times during his annual performance reviews and told him that his performance was not good enough for his advancement in the company. The seasoned quality engineer told my manager that he is content with his job level and that he did not care about advancement. I told my quality group's manager that we should get rid of him as soon as we could. My quality group's manager agreed with me.

I immediately called our human resources director and asked him to come to my office. The three of us discussed the seasoned quality engineer's poor performance, his spiritless behavior, and his termination steps. Our human resources director told us that our company had an at-will employment policy and that we could terminate a nonperforming employee at any time without waiting for a layoff. He also cautioned us that my quality group's manager should document the seasoned quality engineer's poor performance and spiritless behavior during the South Korean trip and discuss the performance document with the employee. This performance document and his annual performance reviews provided legitimacy to his termination and prevented any lawsuits that his termination was discriminatory.

My quality group's manager wrote a performance document for the seasoned quality engineer. Our human resources director and I reviewed the document. After some minor changes, my quality group's manager and our human resources director, together, went over the performance document with the seasoned quality engineer. I heard that even during his performance review, the seasoned quality engineer was spiritless. He accepted all poor performance claims and signed the performance review document. In the late afternoon, our human resources director walked the seasoned quality engineer out the door of our company.

We went through all that hoopla in order to get rid of an underperforming seasoned engineer. My company had a layoff two weeks later. We could have gotten rid of him easily during the layoff process.

Nonperforming and/or underperforming team members are always an issue during the life of a project. Keeping them on the team or getting rid of them has to be weighed very carefully. Risk analysis of your actions has to be thought out in utmost detail. The effects of an underperforming team member can be very destructive in a dynamic team environment.

LESSONS LEARNED FROM THIS PROJECT EVENT

- It is always difficult to spark a fire under lazy and underperforming personnel.
- You have to coordinate with your human resources department and go through the required legal process step by step if you want to terminate personnel.
- It is much easier to clean up underperforming personnel during an official company layoff.

Case 6.8: A Japanese Wedding

One of the important tasks of a project manager is to attend special ceremonies involving your team members. These ceremonies can be birthday parties, weddings, patent presentation banquets, technical society presentations, and so on. As a team leader, one of your main functions is to participate in your team member's celebration events.

One of the most memorable events in my project management career was to attend a Japanese wedding for one of my Japanese team members. He asked me to attend his wedding ceremony as a guest of honor in Tokyo and he also asked me to give a speech during the reception. His wedding ceremony date coincided with my semiannual trip to Japan to check out the progress of my project team there. I accepted his kind offer with excitement. This was my first experience in a Japanese wedding ceremony and reception. I was going to be the guest of honor representing our team and our company and I was going to give a speech.

I had to research how to prepare for this honor. I had to learn what to wear, what kind of gift to get for the couple, and what to say during my speech. He also invited four colleagues from our Japanese team and one colleague from our U.S. team to his wedding ceremony and reception. I learned that the wedding ceremony and reception was going to be a nonreligious one taking place in a banquet room at a very nice hotel in Tokyo. The reception party afterward was going to be in the same banquet room and all my teams' members and I were going to be seated at the same table. I learned that we were required to wear tuxedos with black ties. I decided to stay at the same hotel where the wedding ceremony and reception were. I arranged for a tuxedo rental place through the hotel's concierge. The tuxedo rental place's tailor came to the hotel two days before the event and fitted me with a nice tuxedo. I investigated what the new couple's needs were so that I could get a wedding gift for them. There was no registry process for wedding gifts like we have in the United States. I learned from his colleagues that a flat-screen TV might be a good gift for their new home. I went to Tokyo's electronic stores district and bought a nice 42″ flat-screen Sony TV for them and sent it to their new home with a congratulatory card from me, from our team members, and from our company. Later, I discussed the wedding gift cost issue with human resources. I was able to charge the wedding gift cost to a human resources overhead account instead of my project.

The last thing I had to do was to prepare my speech during the reception. I was allocated five minutes for my speech. I was going to be the last one to give a speech. I learned that the wedding ceremony and reception followed a strict order of events and time allocated for each event was fixed down to the second. The entire reception was going to take exactly two hours and ten minutes with all the speeches, cake cutting, newlyweds' first dance as husband and wife, and so on. I asked one of the engineers from our team in Japan to help me to include several Japanese phrases into my speech. My closing statement was also in Japanese. *Anata wa issho ni, otto to tsuma to shite, naganen, onaji makura no ue ni kenko to kofuku ni kite taisetsu ni ari.* In English it went something like "May you together, as husband and wife, cherish many years to come in health and happiness on the same pillow." I reviewed my speech several times and read it to the engineer who helped me with the Japanese phrases. He said that my Japanese pronunciation was "close to perfect." I was ready for the big event, which was on a Saturday afternoon.

The wedding ceremony and the reception went like clockwork. The bride wore a gorgeous kimono and she had heavy makeup, a wig, and a head covering. The groom wore a standard tuxedo. I gave my five-minute speech very fluently. At the end of my speech, I asked everyone to raise their glasses and toast *kampai* for the new couple. Then the bride went to a changing room to change from her kimono to a Western-style dress. Every guest started to relax, eat, and drink. After dinner, the new couple cut their colossal wedding cake and then they had their first dance as a couple to rock and roll music. Toward the end of the reception, the newly wed couple went around to every table and gave every attendee a gift for sharing their important event.

I attended similar events in Malaysia, South Korea, and in Germany. Attending these special events takes a lot of thought and preparation because you are representing your team and your company.

LESSONS LEARNED FROM THIS PROJECT EVENT

- As project managers, we have to give lots of thought and attention to our team members' special events.
- Especially if you are attending a special event in a foreign country, you have to learn all the do's and don'ts for that event.

Case 6.9: An Engineer Wants to Return to Her Old Job

I had an interesting employee rehire case during my career. I had a quality engineer working on my project team and reporting to the quality engineering department manager. She was a very dedicated and a thorough engineer. She was commuting between her home and work 120 miles every workday. We always chatted about her commute at the beginning of our weekly meetings. We talked about speed traps, getting traffic violation tickets, traffic jams, what are the best hours to drive on the freeway, and so on. I had a good rapport with her. She did not mind the commute and

I thought she enjoyed it. I valued her contributions to my team. One day I got a call from her manager informing me that she gave her notice that she was leaving our company in two weeks.

I was surprised at her departure announcement. I went to her office and expressed my disillusionment. She told me that she was sorry to leave my team. She really enjoyed working on my team. She said that she found a great job very close to her home at a start-up engineering company. Her new job was a perfect fit for her and she would miss my team and also the daily commuting.

I had to scramble to find a replacement for her in the company to join my team. I finally got a novice engineer to replace her. He needed a lot of monitoring and hand-holding. She and my novice engineer were able to interface for about a week so that she could transfer her tasks to him. I also asked her to leave all her engineering books and e-mail files with me regarding my project. Her manager and I gave her a great farewell luncheon. All of my team members attended her luncheon.

After her departure from my company, I still kept in touch with her. We e-mailed each other at least once a month asking how things were going. About four months passed and I received a telephone call from her. She told me that her new job was not what she hoped for. She wanted to quit her job and rejoin my company and especially my project team. I was very surprised to hear her dismay at her new job. Apparently, there was no organizational structure at the new start-up company. She had to take care of everything on her own. Working hours were very long. She was working on average 12 hours a day. Her boss was enforcing unreasonable deadlines on her. All they did was to rush-rush to get a prototype out to their customer so that they could guarantee their next phase of funding. She wanted to return to our more structured and employee-valued environment. I told her that our company had a no-rehire policy, but I promised her that I was going to try my best to get her back.

The next day, I set up a meeting with her old manager and the human resources director. I explained to them in detail the call I had from her. I expressed my favorable views about rehiring her. After an hour of discussion, we came to a just solution to be able to bring her back to our company. She was going to join my team as a consulting quality engineer. The novice engineer would move back to the quality department. She would contribute to my team for the rest of my project, which had another year and a half to go. After a year and a half, the quality department manager would reinstate her as a senior quality engineer into his group. This way we were not going to break the no-rehire rule of our company.

I called her immediately after our meeting and told her our solution for rehiring her. She was ecstatic that she was coming back to work for my company and very grateful for my help. She accepted our proposal to work as a consultant for a year and a half and join the quality group full time afterward. I told her that she would get a formal call in the next day or two from the quality department manager and the human resources director to finalize the details of her return.

Three weeks after her pleading phone call to me, she started to work for me. Her work ethic and contributions to my team were of the highest standard. She was reinstated into the quality group after 18 months on a full-time basis as promised. I thought the company gained an excellent employee by taking her back. We did not break the no-rehire rule of our company, but we had to bend it a little.

A work environment should be like a second family environment away from home. Every employee should be able to talk and express his or her issues and concerns to their managers, upper management, and/or to human resources without any reservations or fears. These issues and concerns can be personal ones, work-related ones, or community-related ones. As managers, our responsibility is to help every employee all we can to make them feel that they are always under our company's family umbrella.

LESSONS LEARNED FROM THIS PROJECT EVENT

- After leaving your job at will from a company, it will be very unlikely for you to go back to your old job.
- Job hopping is an unwritten taboo between competing high technology companies.
- As project managers, we have to help a good person in our team all that we can when that person makes a personal mistake.

Case 6.10: A Deserving Vacation

I had a long-term project to ramp up volume production for a communication chip in Malaysia. I had a good team of engineers in the United States supporting our efforts in Malaysia. I was sending them back and forth from the United States to Malaysia. We were training the Malaysian engineers. They were taking over full responsibility of their assignments after about six months of training. One of the areas where I was having my doubts was the wafer testing in the clean room. There were three young, novice electrical engineers trying to learn and take over all the testing functions such as operator training, tester maintenance, tester upgrading, and tester software development.

I had to send one of my senior test engineers to Malaysia the beginning of November. I assured him that he would only stay there for three weeks and he would be back home by Thanksgiving. He was a strong family man. He had a wife and a 12-year-old son. We put together a detailed three-week agenda for him. We discussed and agreed on all agenda items with the Malaysian engineers. The senior test engineer's progress was going smoothly during the first week of his mission in Malaysia. However, when he saw the reality of the testing environment in Malaysia, he started to add more items to his to-do list that required extensive training. The Malaysian engineers were struggling in the software development phase of the testers. During our daily telephone discussions, I asked him if he could stay another three weeks to complete his extended tasks and skip Thanksgiving at home. He agreed to my proposal. I thanked him for his dedication and I told him that I would strongly emphasize his commitment to our company during his annual review.

Another two weeks passed and Christmas was coming, but my senior test engineer's to-do list was growing instead of shrinking. We again discussed what to do about his stay there. He missed his family and he wanted to return home. I did not have anyone else on my team and not even in the whole company with similar extensive experience to send to Malaysia to relieve him. I had to ask him to extend his stay until his mission was complete. I made him a proposal for his extended stay. I told him if he extended his stay until the end of January and completed his mission, I would treat his wife and his son to a vacation in a place of his choice in Southeast Asia. He was very appreciative of my vacation proposal. He said that he would discuss my all paid vacation proposal with his wife.

The next day during our telephone call, he informed me that he would take my vacation proposal and spend the first week in February on the island of Langkawi at the northwest coast of peninsular Malaysia. Finally, they would get together as a family to relax on a tropical island after three months of separation. He and his wife enjoyed the marine life and beaches. His wife was anxious to absorb some of the Malaysian culture. They were also able to take a week off for his son from his schooling. They chose the Langkawi Island as their vacation spot.

My senior test engineer stayed in the Malaysian plant for three months instead of three weeks as originally planned and he completed his mission with flying colors. He missed Thanksgiving, Christmas, and the New Year holidays at his home. My all expenses paid one-week vacation proposal for him hit the spot. That was his family's first trip to Southeast Asia. They had a great time on Langkawi Island. My gesture cost my project about $4,000, but every penny spent was worth it. He sacrificed his family and his holidays and completed his tasks in Malaysia with exceptional professionalism.

In a project environment, during the course of events, these kinds of unexpected sacrifices could come from any one of your team members. Sometimes these sacrifices could come from people outside of your team. As the project manager, you have to recognize and appreciate these kinds of above and beyond duties. A cash bonus, a gift certificate to a restaurant, a couple of tickets to a sporting event, even a contribution to his or her choice of a nonprofit organization can go a long way.

LESSONS LEARNED FROM THIS PROJECT EVENT

- If a team member has to extend his or her stay in a foreign country for unforeseen reasons to help your project, you should recognize and reward his or her sacrifices accordingly.
- Being away from family for a long time in a foreign country can negatively affect your team member's overall performance.

Case 6.11: Honeymoon Period

I was assigned to lead an offshore oil rig equipment design, build, test, and installation project. The project was to last one year from the start of design to final installation and acceptance on-site in the North Sea. I had a team of eight design and manufacturing engineers. Our customer was in England. I had a two-week vacation preplanned after the third week into the project. I left the project team in the hands of a senior engineer and left for my family vacation. I had a heart-to-heart discussion with my replacement before I left for him to check on the engineers daily and to take care of their needs so that the schedule would not slip. We had on the contract a 5% of total cost penalty for each week of late acceptance on-site. Everyone on my team was very well aware of our tight schedule and of the late acceptance penalty. No one had any slack time for his or her assigned tasks.

I came back after two weeks from my vacation and got a briefing from my replacement project manager regarding the status of all current and completed tasks. I saw that we were behind about a week to two weeks in several tasks. I went around and discussed task-delaying reasons and the issues in detail with every engineer on my team. I saw a relaxed atmosphere in the whole team. They all were behaving like they were on a honeymoon. It was summertime and excessive heat, beaches, surfing, sailing, and outdoor barbecues were giving them all a cozy feeling. My replacement project manager did not do a good job of monitoring and putting adequate pressure on the team members. They all said to me we would catch up eventually and not to worry. I heard the emergency bells ringing in my head. I went to my office to evaluate the whole project task by task and to decide on my course of action.

The next day I called an emergency team meeting. During the meeting, I went over every task with my team. I showed them on the schedule that with the present pace we would be at least one week and at most three weeks late for the acceptance of on-site completion. I emphasized that the progress we had made was not acceptable to our customer nor to our company. I asked everyone for his or her input as to how to catch up and not delay the project by even one day.

There were some great suggestions from the team. I thought the whole team woke up from a summer honeymoon dream. There were six critical tasks that fell behind. Six engineers that fell behind offered to work some extra hours to catch up during the next two weeks. At the same time, other engineers and I were going to give them an extra hand in several minor tasks. I was going to meet with every engineer daily for 15 minutes to discuss the condition of his or her tasks.

The stress levels on the team members were high for the next four weeks. We finally caught up to the critical task on the schedule, which was the internal design review meeting. At the beginning of the internal design review meeting, I praised all my team members for giving extra effort in order to catch up to the schedule. I invited them to a team beach barbecue with their families on Friday afternoon. They all accepted my invitation. We all had a great time at the beach after roller coaster stress levels at work for the last three months.

During the course of a project, stress levels go up and down for every team member. A good project manager has to keep these stress levels as normal as possible without burning out his or her people. It is normal for the stress levels to go up before a critical design review meeting, before a regulatory agency inspection, after an unexpected malfunction of your product, before a final product acceptance event, and so on. However, as the project manager, your important task is to smooth out these stress levels during the course of a project.

I have seen many project teams go through a honeymoon period at the beginning or at the middle of a project. You have to watch for the slacking signs from every team member and take the necessary action to keep the pressure cooker at a constant stress level. It is also a good idea for the project manager not to go on a vacation during the course of a project that has no slack time on its schedule and that has performance penalties in its contract.

LESSONS LEARNED FROM THIS PROJECT EVENT

- A project manager's replacement during his or her absence from a project can have adverse effects on team members.
- It is always difficult to shake off a honeymoon period's relaxed atmosphere in a team environment.
- As project managers, we might have to delay our vacations to after the completion of a project.

Case 6.12: Farewell Luncheon

The computer company that I worked for had a chief operating officer whose top priority was to generate a favorable balance sheet for Wall Street every quarter. When we could not meet our shipment forecasts, he used to ship products that were in our inventory out the door on the last day of the quarter and receive them back as warranty return the next day. If the sales forecast for a particular quarter was down, he used to monitor all travel and extra expenses such as luncheons and in-house birthday parties, and so on. He tracked every penny that was spent.

During tight expenditure periods, we had to get the chief financial officer's approval before going on a trip or before taking someone out to lunch or dinner at company expense. Airplane travel was to be only in economy class. We had strict per diem expense limits depending upon the place we were traveling to. We could not take our customers or colleagues to lunch or dinner without prior approval. Controlling expenses and austerity policies were good for profit and loss management, but the chief operating officer should have given company managers reasonable leeway in managing their budgets.

I had a senior mechanical tool designer on my project team. He was moving to his home state to be close to his aging parents after 15 years of service to our company. He participated in several of my projects during his last 10 years with his highly professional work ethics. My team and I wanted to give him an unforgettable farewell party. However, we were right in the middle of a financial crunch. I had to get every expense preapproved. My team and I decided to throw his farewell party ourselves without going through the expense preapproval process.

I met with each of my team members and asked for their suggestions. First, we decided to give a morning break chocolate cake party around his cubicle. My secretary volunteered to bake the cake. We were going to invite all top management people including the chief operating officer to the morning break party. One of the team members suggested that we get a commemorative plaque for all his contributions to our team. We agreed to chip in $10 each for a silver plaque.

Afterward we planned to take him out to a farewell luncheon at his favorite Mexican restaurant and to give him several presents. I assigned a team member to get the presents before the luncheon. I knew that my tool designer was a skier and a golfer. We decided to get him a pair of ski goggles and half a dozen LED lighted golf balls. The cost for each team member was $16.

The morning break chocolate cake party was well attended. I gave a little speech praising my tool designer and wished him well in his new life. I asked our chief operating officer to present him the silver plaque. The chief operating officer said some inspiring words and did his presentation. It was a great 20-minute get-together and the delicious chocolate cake was all gone. I thanked my secretary on the side for her great cooking skills. I also mentioned to our chief operating officer that we were paying all farewell party expenses from our pockets. He was very tickled to hear that.

Then my team and I took him out to lunch and had outstanding Mexican food in my tool designer's honor. Everyone around the table gave spirit-lifting speeches about him. I gave him his presents and thanked him again for his outstanding contributions to my projects. He was ecstatic about his presents. He gave a gracious farewell speech too thanking each individual on my team and me for coaching, mentoring, and providing assistance all throughout his career at our company. Lunch cost for each team member was $7. Overall we had a great farewell party for my tool designer. The cost of the farewell party for each team member was $33.

The company overall saved a $330 expense. We managed to give a great farewell party to my senior mechanical tool designer without going through the pre-approval process for expenses. All our efforts were for a good colleague and we accomplished everything without any help from the company.

LESSONS LEARNED FROM THIS PROJECT EVENT

- Sometimes you have to be creative and go around strict company rules and policies without breaking any laws.
- As project managers, we have to always show our appreciation for good efforts put into our team by a fellow team member who is leaving the company under favorable conditions.

Case 6.13: Promises to Team Members

As a project manager, my ultimate target was to gain the respect of my team members nationally and internationally. The best way to gain respect was to keep all my promises to team members in a timely fashion. I learned this approach the hard way. Earlier in my project management career I made promises that I could not keep. These unkept promises created conflicts and disharmony in my project teams. A simple promise to upgrade one of my team member's workstation was not fulfilled on time due to my company's budgeting conflicts. My design engineer was livid about my not keeping my end of the bargain in a timely fashion. I had to authorize an upgrade to his workstation instead of waiting for the IT department to act and charged the upgrade to my project.

More conflicting promises arose from things that were outside of my control as a project manager. Examples of these uncontrollable promises were salary increases, bonuses, changing departments, and extra vacation times.

I had a design engineer from our Japanese division working for me in California. I brought him to the United States for two years of extra training and for him to help me in projects dealing with our Japanese customers. He brought his family to the United States too. During his stay in the United States, he still reported to his supervisor in our Japanese division. He was at engineer 2 level. Engineer 2 level was defined according to our Japanese division standards, which was different from the U.S. engineer 2 level ones. He was always complaining about his salary level to me. Our level 2 engineers were making 20% more than what he was making. He was a good and hard working engineer and his contributions were as valuable as his U.S. counterparts. During one of our weekly meetings, I promised him that I would discuss his salary situation with his supervisor and request an increase in his salary. I called his supervisor and negotiated hard with him about increasing his salary by at least 10%. His supervisor would not budge. His supervisor told me that this young Japanese engineer had two more years to go at engineer 2 level. After two years depending on his performance, he could be promoted to engineer 3 level and get a handsome bump in his salary, which would be comparable to U.S. engineer 2 level. My hands were tied. I could not do anything else to keep my promise. I made a promise that I should not have. I should have called his supervisor and discussed his salary increase before promising him anything. I called the young Japanese engineer to my office and explained to him my discussions with his supervisor. I told him that I would give him a very high recommendation for the work he was doing in the United States for me. He could be promoted to engineer 3 level in two years and then could achieve the salary level he was aiming for. He understood his salary situation. He was working for me in the United States under our Japanese division's rules. He continued his good and hard work and he got his promotion on his return to Japan after two years. He called me and thanked me for my very favorable recommendation.

I had another unfulfilled promise early in my career. I had a team of six engineers to design and create software for feasibility studies of industrial investments. We tested and released the software on time and within our budget. During our project closure meeting, I promised my team members good year-end bonuses for their extraordinary efforts. Our feasibility software was being used for every new industrial project planned by our corporation. My six engineers reported to three different managers in our corporation. I talked to every one of them about the success of my team. I emphasized that our corporation was gaining a lot by optimizing investments made to new industrial divisions by using our feasibility software. All managers agreed to recommend handsome year-end bonuses for my team's engineers. In January, all year-end bonuses were announced, but none of my team's engineers got a penny. I was very disturbed and I could not face my team's engineers. I went to see their managers to understand what happened. They all gave me the same story. Due to corporate profit crunch, year-end bonuses were given to very few people. My engineers missed the bonus pot. I had to explain to every one of my team's engineers what happened despite my efforts. I was wrong in raising the hopes of my team's engineers for something that I had no control of.

In another empty promise case, one of the engineers on my team was not happy at all with her supervisor. She wanted to change her department and report to another supervisor whom she thought very highly of. I promised her that I would talk to both supervisors and would help her to switch departments. I discussed her wish with both supervisors and with our human resources director with no success. The department that she wanted to move to had to generate a new opening at her level and her capabilities. Then she had to officially apply for this new job opening. I did not have the authority to accomplish her desired move in any way. Her options were to quit the company or to learn to deal with her supervisor. She chose the second option. She had to endure another three years before her supervisor was assigned to another position.

In one of my design projects, we had a very tight schedule. Our salespeople underbid my project. My project hours were reduced by 25%. My four engineers were putting in 12-hour days and working Saturdays and Sundays to keep up with our project schedule. My team was close to burnout and they were not enjoying their jobs. They were joking with me by saying that they wished they were hourly employees. They would be making at least double their salaries if they were hourly employees. I had to keep them energized and happy. I worked the long hours alongside them. I promised them an extra week of vacation time after the project was completed. I talked to their supervisor in detail. He did not agree with my generous vacation offer. He said that his engineers were salaried personnel and they were judged by the quality and the quantity of their accomplishments and not by the hours that they put in. I was dumbfounded. I did not agree with his assessment of salaried personnel at all. I took it on myself to correct these unfair working conditions. I gave my engineers a day off during the week if they spent a weekend day at the office. I showed these days off as working days on my project. This way I eased their stress levels. In the end, I overran my budget by 9%, but it was all worth it. We were only late by a week to complete a yearlong project. I was apologetic to my team members that I could not give them an extra week of vacation time. They were all appreciative that I leveled their stress levels by a day off during the week.

As I gained experience in project management, I only made promises that I could keep to my team members. I researched thoroughly beforehand whether I could keep my promise. When I gave a time frame for a promise, I always accomplished it within that time frame.

LESSONS LEARNED FROM THIS PROJECT EVENT

- Promises not fulfilled in a timely fashion to team members will create disharmony and underperformance during the execution of your project.
- Do not make a promise to a team member that is beyond your control.
- Always discuss your idea for reward with the supervisor of your team member and obtain his or her consent before announcing it.

Case 6.14: A Critical Team Member Getting Married and Going on a Honeymoon

In the middle of an offshore oil platform equipment design and construction project, one of my critical software design engineers decided to get married and go on a honeymoon. He came to my office one day right in the middle of our project's very high activity period and surprised me by saying that he was going to get married in a month in Mexico and then go on a honeymoon to Australia for three weeks. He was going to be off the project close to four weeks. These surprising events were not planned in my project scheduling at all. He was responsible for designing and generating the software for the control system of the equipment. He was right in the middle of his tasks. I told him that this was quite a change of events in the middle of our project. His absence period coincided with the initial testing of the equipment using his control system. I had no one capable of taking over his tasks. I had to think and find ways to manage his tasks during his absence.

I could not get mad at him or ask him to delay his plans. He was one of my ace engineers. I congratulated him on his decision to get married, but I also told him that he should have planned for his marriage at least six months ago. I told him that I was going to prepare a plan to take care of his responsibilities in his absence. I told him to meet with me again the next day on the subject.

He had four more weeks of work before he left for Mexico. His efficiency was going to drop, as he got closer to his wedding day because of intense activities for his wedding ceremony. The first thing I had to get him to do was to bring the control system software to a preliminary and operable phase before he left. He had to provide me with a preliminary version of the software. He had to leave me with his computer's password and software file locations. I was not going to ask him to release his control software through document control in its preliminary version. He was going to train me on the usage of his software during his last two days in the office. I did not want to get any other team members distracted spending time on his software. Then I was going to ask him to give us a call every morning at 9 a.m. Australian eastern daylight time (3 p.m. Pacific daylight time) so that we could discuss all problems and hiccups that we had encountered while operating the equipment control system software. I did not want to call him and disturb him on his honeymoon every time I had an issue with his software.

I had an hour meeting with him the next day. I laid out my proposed solutions for his absence. He agreed with me that he was going to be able to complete a preliminary version of his software before he left for Mexico. He was not going to be able to complete user instructions for his software by the time he left. He agreed to train me on the usage of his software for two days before he left. He also agreed to call me on Skype Tuesday through Saturday mornings five times a week at the agreed time. He was very appreciative of my understanding of his situation. He told me that one of my project's team members was going to be a groomsman at his wedding.

I checked his progress daily during the next four weeks. He completed as promised a preliminary version of his software before he left for his big day in Mexico. He trained me for two days on all the inputs, outputs, and possible trouble areas of his software. He called me from Australia on the agreed upon call schedule. Some of the calls lasted five minutes, but several of them lasted over an hour. We tried several ways to solve software operating issues while he was live on Skype. With the daily calls, we got along okay in his absence. He completed and released his control software and its user instructions two months after his return from Australia. My team members and I contributed handsomely to get a great present for our newlywed colleague.

Several unexpected events like this one occur during the course of a project. Some project managers get upset and blow their tops off, but this type of behavior does not solve anything. Negative reactions make things worse. You have to be coolheaded, versatile, and firm to find other solutions fast in order to bring the difficult situation under control.

LESSONS LEARNED FROM THIS PROJECT EVENT

- Many surprising and unscheduled events can occur during the execution of your project.
- As project managers, we have to be coolheaded, versatile, and able to orchestrate a viable solution to keep our project moving ahead unharmed.

Case 6.15: A Project Manager Goes on a Sabbatical Leave

I was a senior scientist in a team of several engineers and designers that were assigned to design and build prototypes of a new rotary combustion engine in 18 months. Our team leader was a dedicated automotive engineer and an excellent team leader. Right at the height of the project, he had to take a three-month sabbatical leave to fulfill his compulsory military service. He asked me if I could lead the team during his absence. I accepted the challenge without any hesitation. I knew all the team players well. All tasks were progressing smoothly. I did not see any problems on the horizon. We agreed that he was going to call me twice a week in the evenings to get a briefing about the project. He gave me authorization to sign off on all time cards and all expenses for the project. We had a team meeting and he explained his situation to the team. He introduced me as the interim project manager for the project for the next three months. The next day he left to fulfill his military service obligation.

I started to manage the team without any incidents. The first week passed without a glitch. The project was on track on all cylinders. My management style was different from our project manager. He liked to micromanage every team member to the extreme. On the other hand, I gave a calculated space to team members working under me. I gave a task to a team member and asked for results in a given time frame depending upon the team member's experience and dedication to his or her work.

During the second week, one of the design engineers started to slack off. His behavior was reminiscent of a mouse playing because the cat was gone. His work efficiency dropped drastically. His outside interests increased. He started to take long lunch hours. He called in sick on Mondays. At first I cautioned him verbally. Nothing in his behavior changed. He thought he could get away with it since I was the interim project manager. I discussed his behavior with the project manager during our bi-weekly briefing. He asked me to write a warning letter and review the letter with the design engineer in the presence of a human resources representative. I reviewed the written warning with the design engineer and filed it with human resources. I started to micromanage him and tried to help him get on track and catch up with his tasks. I did not want to take drastic measures and fire him before our project manager returned from his sabbatical leave. Everyone else on the team was performing well. I was patient and limped along with the design engineer for three months.

Our project engineer came back and relieved me from my team management responsibilities. He was also very upset with the project engineer for not completing his tasks as scheduled. Our project manager gave him a written warning too. He was ready to fire the project engineer. I asked the project manager to give me another week to straighten out the project engineer. I told him that the design engineer was very knowledgeable in material science and it would not be easy to replace him in the middle of the project. He agreed with me. I took the project engineer out to lunch to have a heart-to-heart discussion about his work behavior and performance. I told him that he had to pull himself together without any delay and had to improve his work performance or else he had to find another job. I emphasized to him that management was ready to fire him if he did not improve his work behavior and performance fast. He started to share his personal problems with me. He had a new girlfriend who was apparently very demanding. He was prioritizing his new girlfriend before his work responsibilities.

Our two-hour long lunch discussion did the trick. Finally, the gravity of his deteriorating situation at work dawned on him. He started to work harder. He put in many extra hours to catch up with his commitments. Our project manager thanked me for saving the design engineer from being fired. That disruption would have put a dent in the progress of our project.

As project managers, we have to sometimes act as psychologists. We should not take drastic actions on a whim or in a burst of anger. We have to consider all repercussions that an immediate action might cause in our project. A colleague of mine used to always remind me to "measure twice or better three times before you make a critical cut."

LESSONS LEARNED FROM THIS PROJECT EVENT

- Difficulties can arise between you and your team members when you take over a project in the middle of its execution.
- As project managers, we have to consider all options before we make a critical decision.

Case 6.16: Technical Publishing during a Project

I always encouraged my project team members to publish their leading-edge findings in reputable journals as long as their publications did not disclose any intellectual property of our company and of our customers. I also encouraged them to subscribe and to read all technical journals in their fields so that they could stay up to date in their fields of expertise. I asked every team member to share his or her news about technological advances in our weekly team meetings. As engineers we were always in a technology race. As soon as we stopped learning and closed our eyes to the outside world, we would fall behind in our field and we would evaporate. Our publications enhanced our resumes to a higher level and gave us an insurmountable edge over our competition in promotions and in job searches.

In my project management career, I had to provide my team members a fair balance between time spent on writing papers and on doing actual project work. I had a Ph.D. physicist working for me on an advanced magnetic head design project. His knowledge of advanced magnetics was excellent. He spent almost 50% of his working time writing papers for different journals. He was also refereeing submitted papers on several journals during working hours. He came to work exactly at 8 a.m. and left exactly at 5 p.m., not a minute later. He copublished most of his papers with other contributors from my project team. If he did not copublish, he acknowledged all the contributors in his papers. He was a well-respected scientist in his field. I valued his achievements but I had to get more out of him on my project's side and reduce his commitments to publishing during working hours.

I went to his office and had a heart-to-heart discussion about his excess commitment to publication during working hours. I told him that it was okay with me if he spent 10% to 15% of his working hours on publication-related issues. I reminded him that his project tasks in advanced magnetic head design were falling behind. He told me that he was always in a race with other scientists to publish a new idea. He wanted to be the first one to publish a new idea in the scientific world. He also had to get approval from our patent lawyers before submitting his papers. He believed that it was always desirable to have our company's name first in leading journals.

I agreed with all his comments and left his office without a resolution regarding his time spent on writing and refereeing papers. I had to think hard not to antagonize him and get a fair resolution to our problem. I did not want to go to his boss and complain about the situation at hand. I had to deal with him myself and find a fair solution. I thought about a middle-ground solution for a couple of days. Then I called him to my office in order to propose and negotiate my solution. I told him that he could spend all the time he wanted on publishing and refereeing papers as long as he put in an honest 32 hours of work on my project every week. I gave him freedom in 20% of his weekly working hours to do whatever he wanted to do in publishing. If he wanted to spend more time in publishing, he had to do it after 5 p.m. at work or at home. He could not argue with my proposal. He told me that I was trying to put brakes on his publishing efforts. I emphasized that my project's tasks were more important than his publishing efforts. I reminded him that our company could only survive, if we were the leader in our products, not in publishing. Finally, he came around and reluctantly accepted my proposal. I told him that in dire situations such as a deadline, he could spend more work time for publishing as long as he notified me. This fine loophole gave him more confidence in our relationship. Finally, he started to spend 32 hours per week on my project's tasks.

Specialists and/or scientists can be very moody and demanding in a team environment. As a project manager, you need their expertise. You have to treat them with respect. You have to create a flexible boundary with their needs and with your project's requirements. If you become a hard-liner with such people, your project will suffer in the end.

LESSONS LEARNED FROM THIS PROJECT EVENT

- Getting a team member to focus on your project's tasks can be challenging when that team member has a lot of other interests besides your project.
- Your flexibility in solving a difficult case regarding a team member will benefit your project in the long run.

Case 6.17: Team Atmosphere after Vacations and Holidays

As global project managers we have to know every team member's vacation plans in advance. We have to know all national holidays of the countries we are dealing with. We have to know all religious holidays that each one of our team members and countries are observing. Religious holiday observance days might get very confusing, if you are dealing with multi-ethnic countries like India and Malaysia. It is always a must to include all these events into your project schedule at the initial stage of your planning. You might come across many surprises that can affect your project's critical tasks and deliverables.

In one of my project teams, I had a novice engineer who could not get into a work mood easily after he came back from holidays. He was still dreaming about turkey dinners, apple pies and ice cream, a Christmas gift he got, and New Year's celebrations. He was going around discussing his experiences during the holidays in detail with child-like excitement with his colleagues. I had to micromanage him daily after the holidays so that he could get back to his work and start focusing on his tasks. After a couple of holidays, he started to act more professionally and discussed his holiday experiences with his teammates only during breaks.

This novice engineer took his two-week vacation after a year of employment and went to Tahiti with his girlfriend. After he got back he acted like a lost soul under lots of stress. He could not switch easily from a relaxed atmosphere to the rhythm of organized work. His e-mails and his phone messages accumulated quite a bit during his two weeks of absence. He did not know which task to tackle first. He came to my office and asked for my help. I told him to first review all his e-mails and phone messages and jot down important ones and ones that needed action and response from him. Then I asked him to come back to my office with his list the same day. He came back and we together reviewed his action items list and prioritized every item on it. We also put completion dates for each action item. This kind of personalized help showed my novice engineer how to deal with numerous action items on his to-do list after a relaxing vacation. He appreciated my guidance and thanked me a lot for easing his stress level. He went on to become a very organized and productive engineer in two years. After two years, I recommended him to be promoted to an engineer 2 level. He received his promotion. He was very grateful to me and he always wanted to work on my projects.

In an opposite case, an engineer from our Malaysian facility was working on my project in California. I brought him to California for a six-month period to help me in several tasks in my volume production ramp-up project and to be trained in certain inspection methods. One day he came to my office and asked if I could send him back to Malaysia for a week to see his family during a religious holiday that was coming up in 10 days. His request came to me by surprise at a very high activity phase of our project. I told him that it would put a big dent in the progress of our project if he were gone for a week. I could not outright reject his request. I had to do all I could to find a way to send him home for a week to spend his important religious holiday with his family. I told him that I would try to bring in another engineer to fill in for him for a week. I also told him that I could not pay for his trip expenses from my project's budget. I promised him a response in a day.

I discussed my Malaysian engineer's holiday request and my project's dire need for backup engineering manpower for a week with our quality engineering manager and got one of his engineers to help me. I immediately gave the good news to my Malaysian engineer that he could leave our team for a week. Somehow he found a cheap round trip ticket in a short time and went home for his religious holiday. After he got back, he worked very hard and long hours on my project team to pay me back his gratitude.

Unexpected vacation and holiday requests from team members can occur during the course of a global project. Vacations and holidays tend to bring instability to the progress and atmosphere of a project. As project managers, we have to deal with them in a timely fashion and try to smooth out their ripple effects.

LESSONS LEARNED FROM THIS PROJECT EVENT

- It takes awhile and your continual guidance to get some of your team members into an effective working mood after holidays and vacations.
- Unexpected vacation or holiday requests can come from your team members. You have to deal with these requests in a positive manner.

Case 6.18: Project Team Member's Maternity Leave

Maternity leave can hit your project team any time. You have to restructure your team and get new personnel reinforcements in a timely fashion in order not to affect the progress of your project.

In a new wafer factory setup project, I had a very talented female engineer on my team. She was very experienced in experimental design and in industrial statistics. She was designing all qualification experiments for new equipment along with equipment engineers who were cognizant of wafer processes and then analyzing resulting data with them. She came to my office one day and told me that she was four months pregnant. She had already talked with our human resources group. She was very excited about her first child. She was planning to take off a week before her due date, which was predicted by her doctor, and she was going to take a total of 12 weeks for maternity leave. She was going to have her full salary and her full health benefits during her maternity leave. She was also going to have full job protection. She wanted to come back and continue to work on my team after her maternity leave was over. She also would not be able to fly after her sixth month of pregnancy, which was going to be in two months. I congratulated her and wished her a healthy pregnancy. I asked her to think about how to replace her temporarily for 12 weeks. I asked her to get together with me on the subject in a week.

I considered my options too during the week. I analyzed all her upcoming tasks. Her maternity leave was occurring right in the thick of things in my project. I had to find a reliable replacement for her fast so that the two of them could spend a month together before she went on her leave. She came to my office the following week to discuss her temporary replacement. We could not agree on an internal replacement. No one in our company had the broad and in-depth experimental design skills that she possessed. We decided to go outside to a consulting firm. This consulting firm had given her lots of training in the past. We called the consulting firm and set up a face-to-face meeting. We agreed on a senior consultant to come and help us during her maternity leave. This senior consultant was at one time her training instructor. He was very expensive, but he was the right person for the job. He agreed to start a month before her maternity leave for a phase-in period for her tasks. I asked my purchasing department to put together a contract with the consulting firm. We had to cover his travel, lodging, and meal expenses too. The senior consultant's expenses were going to put a huge dent into my project's cost performance. I went to my upper management and negotiated to charge to my project only the amount equal to my engineer's salary. The rest of the consultant's expenses were to be absorbed into the company overhead. That was the just way of splitting the consultant's cost to my project.

The consultant started to work on my team along with her a month before her maternity leave. The phase-in and phase-out process was smooth. She gave birth to a healthy boy on the day predicted by her doctor. My team and I sent her hospital congratulatory flowers. I talked with her on the phone and discussed her and the baby's health. Everyone was doing great.

Two months passed after her birth, I got a phone call from our human resources group informing me that she wanted to take off another six weeks after her maternity leave was over for baby bonding. She was going to have 50% of her salary, her full health benefits, and her full job protection during this baby bonding period. This was quite a shock to me. She did not even call me to discuss her decision to extend her maternity leave. My human resources director told me that she had the right for this baby bonding leave under California law.

I discussed the six-week baby bonding extension with the senior consultant. He said he could not extend his contract because he already had other commitments. He had three more weeks left on his contract with us. During these six weeks, all her tasks were on the critical path of my project. I had to scramble again to find a replacement for her for another six weeks. I decided to groom a willing engineer internally for my team. Internal grooming was also beneficial for my company in the long run. I discussed the issue with all engineering departments' heads. Two names came up as possible candidates. I interviewed both engineers. I decided to give a novice and ambitious mechanical engineer a try. He spent three weeks next to the senior consultant. I called my female engineer at home to discuss the bind I was in. She offered to help my new engineer on the phone from home. We limped through six weeks of her baby bonding period. Finally, my female engineer returned to her tasks after 18 weeks. During this chaotic period in my project, my company gained another bright engineer who went on to become an expert in experimental design and in industrial statistics.

LESSONS LEARNED FROM THIS PROJECT EVENT

- When a maternity leave request comes to you, always bring your human resources department into the picture to learn all federal, state, and company rules, regulations, and options.
- You have to be ready for surprises during a maternity leave so that your project does not suffer.

Case 6.19: Shelf Life of Photoresists in Wafer Fabrication

In wafer fabrication of magnetic heads the photoresist played a very important role. As the photoresist aged, its sensitivity to light exposure and its light absorption characteristics changed. This variability in turn affected our product's steep wall profiles. Our product lost wall edge acuity. Therefore, all of a sudden lots of wafer scraps started to occur. This phenomenon occurred intermittently in our wafer fabrication when I was heading the engineering group. I had several meetings with my photolithography engineers. We could not determine the cause of the degrading edge acuity phenomenon. We did lots of design of experiments, but we could not pin the yield drop to the age of the photoresist used in the factory.

One of my quality engineers in wafer fabrication suggested my team perform an experiment with the age of photoresist versus steep wall edge acuity. Everyone on the team agreed to these experiments. I assigned the quality engineer who suggested the experiment along with a photolithography engineer to perform the required tests in two weeks. They ran experiments with one-, two-, three-, four-, five-, and six-month-old photoresists. They found out that steep wall edge acuity in our products started to degrade when the photoresist was older than three months. They also ran confirmation experiments to verify these results.

I immediately issued a memorandum to all shifts in wafer fabrication not to use any photoresists that were older than three months. We had another problem with the photoresist containers. The manufacturing date of the photoresist was indicated on a sticker by the manufacturer, but this sticker very often fell off the container. So we sometimes had no idea when the photoresist was manufactured. I called the photoresist manufacturer with our receiving inspection and purchasing managers. We asked them to put permanent laser markings on every photoresist container identifying the lot number and the manufacturing date.

The photoresist manufacturer agreed to our container markings request. Two weeks after our telephone discussion, we started receiving photoresist containers that were permanently marked with the lot number and the manufacturing date.

The photoresist usage expiration date had to be on every container. I discussed this issue with our stockroom manager. We decided to laser scribe usage expiration dates on the body of the container in large fonts. We kept the photoresist in special storage rooms with temperature, 5°C to 10°C, and relative humidity, 30% to 50%, control. Upon my request, all stockroom personnel were instructed by their manager not to issue to production any photoresist containers that were over the usage expiration date. They were also instructed to dispose of any containers that were over the usage expiration date.

With all the steps taken to control the useful life of the photoresist, our product's steep wall edge acuity became very stable. We did not have any intermittent out-of-specification wall profiles. Our wafer scraps due to out-of-specification wall profiles decreased tremendously.

We spent months to find the cause for our steep wall profile defects. We performed numerous full factorial design-of-experiments with two or three factors and each factor having two or three levels. None of these complicated, time-consuming, and expensive experiments provided us with any reliable solution.

The photoresist useful life effects on steep wall profile were not even suggested by one of my photolithography engineers. The suggestion came from one of my quality engineers. She was not at all involved with our photolithography processes. She was a quality engineer in our plate and etch group. During our weekly engineering team meeting, I praised her for suggesting the solution to one of our mind-boggling problems. I also gave her a handsome bonus during our annual review. I patiently learned to listen and evaluate all suggestions that were proposed during our engineering team meetings. Being a good listener provided my team members with upbeat empowerment and helped us find solutions to difficult issues in our wafer fabrication.

LESSONS LEARNED FROM THIS PROJECT EVENT

- A good solution to a nagging engineering issue can come from unexpected sources.
- As project managers, listening and evaluating everyone's input to a problem increases our chances of success.

Case 6.20: Excessive Meetings

I was leading a project with a U.S. and overseas team in Malaysia to set up a manufacturing plant there. My U.S. team consisted of 12 engineers split equally into design, manufacturing, test, and quality subteams. I had 12 Malaysian engineers based in Penang as counterparts of my U.S. team. We had weekly teleconferences to bring everyone on the team up to date regarding the tasks that everyone was working on. It took us two hours every Monday afternoon (Tuesday morning in Malaysia) to go over all the tasks. It gave every engineer about five minutes on average to present the status of his or her task responsibilities.

We were spending 48 man-hours a week on this teleconference meeting. Everyone was waiting for his or her turn. Some engineers were twiddling their thumbs during the presentations that they had no interest in. Some engineers were busy with their laptops. Some Malaysian engineers were not at the meeting when their turn came up. There was a lot of wasted time during these teleconference meetings. It was an inefficient way to manage a meeting. I decided to take some action to correct the situation.

I talked with my different subteams in the United States and in Malaysia about improving the weekly teleconference meeting. We brainstormed several ideas to improve the efficiency of our weekly status meeting. The best idea came from an engineer in Malaysia. She proposed that we break up the meeting into four half-hour segments, namely design, manufacturing, test, and quality segments. During the design segment, only the design engineers would attend the meeting. During the manufacturing segment, only the manufacturing engineers would attend the meeting. During the test segment, only the test engineers would attend the meeting. During the quality segment, only the quality engineers would attend the meeting. If there were any issues crossing the subteam groups, I would record them as action items in the meeting minutes and a particular issue would be handled by e-mail or by telephone by its action item owner. If any one of the team members were interested in a certain task in a different subteam, he or she could review the released meeting minutes from document control.

I issued the new weekly teleconference meeting process. From 4 p.m. to 4:30 p.m. (U.S. Pacific time zone), it was the design task group's turn, from 4:30 p.m. to 5 p.m., it was the manufacturing task group's turn, from 5 p.m. to 5:30 p.m., it was the test group's turn, and from 5:30 p.m. to 6 p.m. it was the quality group's turn. I also rotated the groups' turns every two months so that one task group did not get stuck with the late afternoon meeting time in the United States or the early morning meeting time in Malaysia. I also had a monthly half-hour general project status teleconference meeting for all team members, domestic and international.

This new communication setup worked very well all throughout the project for two years and we saved about 75% man-hours that were being wasted during the weekly status meetings. On top of that, engineers were not bored during the meeting. They came into the meeting room, gave their presentation, and left the meeting room in half an hour. Sometimes there were shifts in presentation timing. If a subteam's presentation ran over half an hour, I informed the other subteams about the delay and they showed up at the new modified presentation time in the conference room. My counterpart in Malaysia did the same thing.

Meetings are the backbone of a project. They have to be standardized and managed properly so that a precious team member's time is not wasted; the team member is not bored, and he or she contributes constructively during his or her presence in the meeting. Especially in large team groups, as it was in this case, breaking up a meeting into smaller subgroups can be very effective.

LESSONS LEARNED FROM THIS PROJECT EVENT

- Project meetings can accumulate lots of wasted team members' time.
- Plan efficient project meetings and make sure that your team members around the world are not twiddling their thumbs and they do not look bored during a meeting.

Case 6.21: First Article Mishap

I was heading the project of designing, manufacturing, and testing a new generation of battery-powered electric buses. Forty-foot long electric buses provided four and a half hours of stop-and-go level terrain travel on a single charge fully loaded with 80 passengers. The electric buses were for a mall shuttle operation. My team was getting ready for the first article acceptance meeting that was scheduled to start on a Monday and was supposed to last for three days. On Friday morning before the start of the first article acceptance meeting, my manufacturing manager brought the first article bus to the charge station in our plant to charge its batteries. The charging operation took about eight hours. We were running around like our heads were cut off to complete last minute finishing touches and tasks for the Monday meeting. We were all tired and were looking forward to a restful weekend before the big Monday presentation. All my team members and I had been working 70-hour weeks for the last month to prepare the first article for this crucial acceptance meeting.

At 4 p.m. on Friday, I unplugged the battery charger eagerly and started to drive the bus to its presentation spot. There was a short steel post in front of the charge station hidden behind the bus. While backing the bus out of the charge station, I ran the rear side of the bus into the steel post. One of the side rear windows broke and there was minor bodily damage too. It was my mistake to rush to drive the bus to its presentation spot. I knew where the steel post was and I thought I was clearing it during my maneuver. I was so mad at myself for rushing and causing this damage to the bus right before the first article acceptance meeting.

I immediately called a meeting with our manufacturing manager and our body shop personnel. The meeting was held at the damaged rear of the first article bus. I told my team that I was devastated by my mistake and I asked them if the damage was fixable by Monday. We all assessed the damage and agreed that the damage was fixable before Monday's meeting. We decided that three body shop technicians would be needed to fix the damage during the weekend. I asked my team who would volunteer for the weekend overtime repair task. Three out of six technicians volunteered immediately. I told them that I would be at the plant too along with them during the weekend and bring breakfast and lunch for them. My gesture was received very favorably. We were able to replace the broken window easily with another one. The body damage took most of the repair time. The body damage was repaired by straightening the surface sheet metal and then painting over it during Saturday and Sunday.

The first article electric bus was ready for the acceptance meeting at 9 a.m. Monday morning. The fresh paint at the rear of the bus was not even dry. I was afraid to drive the bus to the presentation site. I let my manufacturing manager do the honors. For three days, the first article acceptance meeting went well. Our new generation of battery electric bus got excellent grades from our customer's representatives. They accepted our battery electric bus with minor modifications.

I told our customer's representatives of what happened on Friday. They were amazed that we were able to work all weekend to get the bus fixed and ready in top shape. Our customer was very appreciative of our performance. After the last meeting, they took my whole team of 20 people out to dinner.

These kinds of mishaps happen more often than not while preparing for critical meetings or deadlines in a project. Overworked and overtired team members become prone to mistakes and accidents. As a project manager, I had to watch myself and my team members for fatigue and for burnout conditions. We had to slow down and take a break from running a 100 miles an hour. One solution would have been to delay Monday's first article meeting for a couple of days.

LESSONS LEARNED FROM THIS PROJECT EVENT

- You have to control your pace and fatigue level and your team members' pace and fatigue level when you are preparing for a crucial event for your project.
- It might be wiser to postpone a crucial project event than to burn out yourself and your team members preparing for it.

Index